THEY FOLLOWED THE PIPER

LEE HULTQUIST

LOGOS INTERNATIONAL
PLAINFIELD, NEW JERSEY

Some of the names in this story have been
changed to protect the privacy of individuals
involved.

Dedicated to all those families
whose lives have been touched by the cults

Special thanks to Charlotte Allen for using her beautiful gift of encouragement to start me and keep me going.

As you relive with us my meeting with the "Children of God" and the year of mental, spiritual and emotional turmoil that followed, it is my hope that the very real danger of the cults will be revealed to you. But more than that, I pray that the Holy Spirit will enlighten your heart and mind to the reality that God is with His people in every circumstance. He is utterly dependable. "And we know that all things work together for good to them that love God, to them who are the called according to his purpose" (Rom. 8:28).

As the Lord healed and restored me, He led our family into a ministry with others who had similar experiences with cults. Hopefully, this book will carry that ministry further and will be a testimony to the fact that those who trust the Lord shall not be allowed to follow the piper.

Cyndi Hultquist

Chapter 1

It was a hot July night in our quiet suburb when the phone rang, startling us out of a sound sleep. Late night calls always scared me, and as I turned on the lamp, Glen fumbled for the phone.

The caller was Bo Morris, a friend of our eighteen-year-old daughter Cyndi. Cyndi was sharing an apartment with two other girls, Brenda and Patty, during the summer quarter at a small Christian college in Cleveland, Tennessee. Bo and four friends had rented a big house a block away from the girls. The boys watched out for them, and drove them to and from their jobs in the evening.

After talking briefly with Bo, Glen turned to me. "Lee, Bo just got back to school after the Fourth of July break, and he says Cyndi is missing. She's taken all of her things, and left with a group called the 'Children of God.' " I sat up in bed, wide awake now, fear gripping me like a vise.

"I'll go downstairs to the extension phone, Lee. You'll want to hear what Bo is saying," Glen said.

Both of us listened while Bo tried to explain who these people were. "I don't want to upset you," he said, "but this is a really weird group." The concern in his voice came through, and I felt he was trying to soften the shock of this news for us.

"Tell us what you know about the group, Bo."

"These kids call themselves Christians, and they live in communes. They forsake their families and all earthly

1

possessions, and make their living by handing out tracts and asking for donations. You've probably seen them at the airport. They're the ones who hand out those little comic book tracts."

"Yes," Glen said, "I've seen them around."

Bo said, "I'm worried. Sometimes you don't hear from kids again after they join the group. They're usually sent to another state so their families can't locate them. The Children of God have communes all over the country, and even in Europe."

"How do you know so much about them?" I asked.

"I've talked to some of them on the street, and I had a long talk with one of the leaders. I think they're really off base as far as the Scriptures go. They started out pretty straight, I guess, but they seem to have become perverted in the past few years. The guy that I talked to told me about mass marriages that may last for only a night or a few weeks. The leader, David Berg, or Moses, as he is called, is said to have several wives at a time. His sons also have several wives."

"Cyndi wouldn't fall for such a thing," I said. "She would be able to see through that kind of thing just as you have. She knows the Bible too well to believe such false teaching."

"This is really a slick group, though. They tell you all the right things at first. You ask them if they're saved, and they tell you that they're born-again believers. They come on so straight, that you really believe that they're true Christians at first. Then when you get into the word with them, you find that their leader has changed some of the Scriptures to suit his own purposes. I've read some Mo letters that were real garbage. It's become a sexual thing, really."

"How long has Cyndi been missing?" Glen asked.

"I got back in town about an hour ago, and came over to the apartment, thinking the girls would still be up, even though it was almost midnight. Brenda was here, and she told me Cyndi was gone. When she came back from the evening church service, Cyndi's clothes and everything had been moved out. She didn't leave a note or anything. That's just not like Cyndi. You know how the girls always check in and out with each other, and always know where the others are."

Brenda got on the phone and told us that since she returned from her trip, she had seen Cyndi only once when she came in with two young men who were from the Children of God. Cyndi told her they had been on a picnic.

"I was worried," Brenda told us. "Cyndi didn't spend the night at the apartment, and she didn't call or anything. She's just not the type to do something like that. Patty and I talked about calling you, but we decided to wait until Bo came back today, and ask him what to do. Then when I came home this evening and found that her stuff was gone, I really got worried. She just didn't seem right when I saw her earlier. She seemed—funny."

"What do you mean, funny?" I asked.

"It's hard to describe. She had this funny look in her eyes. They were glassy, like she was on drugs or something. I know she doesn't use drugs," she added quickly, "but that's what I thought of when I saw her. She worried me the way she was talking, too."

"How was she talking?" Glen asked.

"Oh, I don't know, just kind of mad at the whole world, and school and churches and everything. We all bad-mouth the way things are run sometimes, but this was different. Like she had a bunch of stuff put in her head, or something. Patty and I didn't know what to do, so we just waited for Bo. I hope we didn't do the wrong thing. We never dreamed she would join them."

"You did what you thought best, Brenda," I said. "Don't you feel responsible or guilty. We'll get this all straightened out, don't worry."

Brenda gave the phone back to Bo.

"When did you talk to her last?" Bo asked.

"I talked to her on the phone the day you left town," I said. "I was a little concerned about her being alone in the apartment for so many days, so I called to ask her if I could drive up and get her to bring her home for the weekend. She seemed a little

3

depressed, but she said she couldn't come home. She was scheduled to work, and she couldn't let her boss down."

"I'm going to Chattanooga to talk to some of the 'true brothers' on the street, and see if I can find the commune," Bo said. "They usually keep the location of the colony secret, and only give it out to people who are real interested, and may join the group. I'll call you back in a few hours and let you know what I've found out."

"Good," Glen said. "Call us no matter what time it is."

"Don't worry," he assured us. "I'll find her, if I have to join the Children of God myself to do it. I'll find her, and I'll bring her out." With that, Bo's voice broke. "I'm sorry," he said. "I'm just so worried about her. I love her, and don't want her to get mixed up in something like this."

Glen said, "Bo, just locate the colony, and we'll come up there first thing in the morning and talk to Cyndi and find out what this is all about."

"You don't understand," Bo insisted, his voice shaky. "They probably won't let you talk to her. She's virtually a prisoner. They have her mind anyway. I've seen what they do to people. It's heavy."

I said, "Promise me that you won't join them. We don't want you among the missing too."

I got a half-hearted promise from him that he wouldn't join the group, but it worried me that Bo was thinking along those lines.

We prayed together on the phone, asking God to protect Cyndi, and to help Bo locate her. Then we hung up, not realizing that we were just beginning to experience the most bizarre and frightening year of our lives.

4

Chapter 2

Glen and I had heard about strange cults and sects, and the ways that they enticed young people to join. But neither of us had for a moment ever seriously thought that one of our children would get involved with one of them. We had always seen our family as a steady, solid thing, and never imagined that anything like this would ever happen in our home.

Ours was a marriage for keeps. An old-fashioned, for-better-or-worse kind of commitment, with Jesus Christ as the third person in our relationship.

We had had our six children in ten years, working together to take care of the sometimes overwhelming job of caring for so many little people.

Glen was what I called a "liberated" man. He had been big man on campus in high school, and excelled in most sports. He played varsity basketball three years in high school, and four years in college. He went to engineering school on a scholarship won for proficiency in science and mathematics.

Glen was confident enough of his masculinity not to define roles as feminine or masculine. He was strong enough to be gentle, and he enjoyed our babies and played with them as much as I did. He was the youngest child in his family, and had never been around young children much as he was growing up, so I'd often marveled at how good he was with even the youngest baby.

I always felt Glen's confidence came from having such a

stable, loving Christian home as a child. His parents were of Swedish descent. The traditions and customs were taught to the children as they grew up, and the holidays were particularly festive. Though Glen had been born during the depression, and money was not abundant, he never felt poor. Like most people on dairy farms in the Midwest, they always had plenty to eat, and life was simple and happy.

I had never known the security of a stable family as a child. My grandmother died when I was eight years old, and after that I stayed in the county children's home, and then foster homes. I suppose it was this background that made me so determined to provide a good home life, and I poured my all into being the best wife and mother I could possibly be. I wanted my children to have the stability and love I felt every child deserved.

Glen and I are very different in temperament and background, but we got along well. My weaknesses and strengths were compensated for and complemented by Glen's strengths and weaknesses. We had our ups and downs like most couples, and there were times when we both wished the other would get lost, but we took our problems to the Lord, and we worked at our marriage.

And Cyndi. She certainly wasn't the kind of girl who would leave to join a commune without even talking about it first. She just wasn't that kind of girl. She discussed everything with us, including boyfriends. She and Bo were very close. They had been singing together in churches and at school and were very popular, especially with the younger children. There was nothing at all that would indicate that Cyndi was in any way angry enough to consider leaving her family and friends behind and transferring her loyalty to a strange new group of people. But now, for some reason, she had.

After saying good-bye to Bo, Glen came back upstairs. He looked worried as he walked into the bedroom. He sat on the bed next to me, and taking my hand in his said, "Don't worry, everything is going to be okay. We'll go to Tennessee tomorrow and we'll find Cyndi.

"We'll find out what this is all about. Maybe we won't have to go anywhere. Maybe Bo will locate her tonight, and she'll be back at her apartment by morning. We'll just wait for Bo to call back."

We were trying to talk ourselves out of worrying, but it was pretty hard. If her clothes and all of her things had not been moved out of the apartment, I wouldn't have been so worried, but moving out seemed so decisive, so final.

"Maybe the group Cyndi is with is not the same one Bo knows so much about," I said. "There are so many groups of that kind around now. Maybe this is a different group. Just a bunch of Christian kids living together in a commune with a real ministry, and valid leadership. What do you think, Glen?"

"I really don't know what to think. It sure is out of character for Cyndi to do something like this."

"It really is."

"Have you talked to her much lately?" Glen asked. "Has she seemed troubled or anything?"

I tried to think back on the conversations we'd had recently. "I can't think of anything unusual at all," I said. "She seemed happy and full of life. Bo seems to be her main topic of conversation right now. It's Bo and I this, and Bo and I that. Just the usual things a girl talks to her mother about. If she was troubled about anything, I think she would have talked to me about it. I think I would have sensed it, too."

She had just been home two weeks before, and she was the same old Cyndi. Talking a mile a minute, making plans, going places. A group from school had come down for the weekend to stay with us. They had gone rafting down the river and attended church with us. Everything was okay then, I was sure.

Bo called back after several hours, sounding very discouraged.

"I've talked to quite a few people in Cleveland, and in Chattanooga," he told us. "The Children of God have been seen witnessing in the area this past week, but no one seems to

7

know where the commune is. It could be either here in Cleveland, or in Chattanooga. I went to the police station, and they don't know where the commune is, either. I gave everyone I talked to a description of Cyndi, and they all said they'd keep an eye out for her and get in touch with me if they saw her."

Glen told Bo we would be up there in the morning, just as soon as we could get there. We thanked him for calling us, and for looking for Cyndi, and we hung up.

Glen turned off the lights, and we lay there trying to sleep. It would be light in a couple of hours, and we would have a big day ahead of us. I didn't know how I could sleep with my child missing, but I was going to try.

I lay there, my mind going over the events of the evening. So many questions came to my mind. How had Cyndi met this strange group of people? What could persuade a stable, sensible Christian girl to just go off and leave without a word to anyone? It all seemed so incredible to me. Had she had something upsetting happen in her life during the past few days, or weeks that we didn't know about? Questions, questions, but no answers.

I lay there, trying to block out the questions, and thoughts from my mind. Suddenly, I was aware of a light in the room. At first I thought I was dreaming. There by my bed, right next to me, was a clear, pure light that seemed to be surrounded by a cloud, or a mist. I just stared at the light. It was so beautiful. I had never seen anything like it before.

There seemed to be a presence in the light. Though it was silent, it seemed to speak to me of peace and comfort. It was as if the Lord himself was saying to me, "I'm here with you. I have this whole situation under my control. Nothing can separate you from my love. Trust me." Peace just flowed over me, and I had the assurance that everything was truly in God's hands.

I reached over and took Glen's hand. He was awake too. "Do you see that?" I whispered.

He turned toward me. "What?"

"That light."

"I don't see anything. It's so dark in here I can't see anything."

"There's a light right here by the bed." I wanted so much to share it with him.

"I can't see anything," Glen spoke softly. "But I feel such peace in this room. It's like the Lord is here, comforting us, and reassuring us."

"Oh, Glen, it's so beautiful."

The light faded, and I lay there, awed by the beauty of what I had so briefly seen. What could this mean? I was not one to dream dreams or see visions. I was much too practical and realistic to believe in such things, but there it was. Tears flooded my eyes, and I lay there in Glen's arms, assured and comforted in a way that goes beyond anything this world or any person could offer.

I thought of the verse of Scripture that says, "My peace I give unto you; not as the world giveth, give I unto you." I couldn't know then that the Lord was preparing me for a year of trials so great, I would have to remember this night, and hold fast to His reassuring presence.

Chapter 3

We awoke at dawn after just a few hours of sleep. There was so much to do before leaving. I would have to make arrangements to leave the five younger children, and Glen would have to cancel business appointments.

I made myself a cup of coffee, and tried to get my thoughts organized so I wouldn't forget anything. I made a list of things I would have to do, then woke the children.

Lisa, our fifteen-year-old, would have to take charge for the day. Lisa was not the most enthusiastic babysitter, but I knew she would rise to the occasion and take good care of the younger children.

I told the children about the call from Bo, trying to make it sound casual. "I'm sure we'll find her," I said. I didn't want them worrying, but they looked concerned when I told them. Our kids really loved each other, and were close. They fought like mad sometimes, but they would defend each other when one of them got in trouble.

Thirteen-year-old Julie was scheduled to leave for Bible camp that morning. Julie's friend Candi was going for the first time, and the girls had been making plans for weeks about what they were taking to wear and what equipment to bring. Julie tended to worry about things, and I hoped this news of Cyndi being gone would not spoil her camp experience. Camp was the highlight of the summer, and I wanted it to be just as special this year.

Julie's ride came, and I told Candi's mother about Cyndi being missing. As I stood there in the driveway, after putting luggage in the Harrisons' car, it sounded strange as I said, "Cyndi is missing." My voice had a hollow ring. Candi and her mother looked concerned, and said they would be praying for all of us. I kissed Julie good-bye, telling her she was not to worry. "Just forget about it, and have a good time," I said. "I know we'll find her, and I'll write to you tomorrow, telling you all about it."

She said, "I've prayed about it, and now I'm going to forget it."

She looked very determined as she said it. I could see she had thought it over, and come to a logical conclusion, and made a decision.

Amy had been across the street, spending the night with her friend Melanie Parker. The Parkers were close friends, and the children spent their time almost equally at each other's homes.

I hadn't told Amy about Cyndi being missing yet, and I shared briefly with Irene about the call we'd gotten in the middle of the night.

"Just let Amy stay," Irene said. "If you're not back by this evening, I'll just have her spend the night here."

Irene told me she would check with Lisa to see if she needed anything. It sure was nice to have friends to turn to at a time like this.

That left eleven-year-old Wendy, and eight-year-old Eric for Lisa to take care of. "That's not too bad," I thought. Eric had a tendency to forget to tell people where he was going, but I was sure he would stay home and be good for Lisa.

Wendy spent all her waking hours at the pool a block away. She was perpetual motion. When she wasn't in the water, she was doing gymnastics. Earlier in the year she had broken her arm very badly. After surgery, and three months in a cast, I was trying to get her to slow down a bit. I just wouldn't worry about her getting hurt again while I was gone. I just had to trust them all to the Lord. Even Wendy.

Lisa was worried about Cyndi, and I could tell she was upset. She was like Glen in so many ways. She was blonde like me, but she had her father's reserved disposition. When she got worried, she got quiet. She was very quiet now. I walked over to her, and put my arm around her.

"Don't worry," I said. "Everything is going to be all right. We'll find Cyndi and we'll probably be back late tonight. Do you think you can take care of everything here?"

"Sure, I can handle it. The kids will be good. It's just Eric and Wendy. That's not hard."

"Be sure to keep track of Eric, okay? Don't get engrossed in a book, or telephone conversation and forget about him. You know how he wanders off sometimes."

"I'll keep him with me, don't worry. I'll take him to the pool for a while this afternoon, and I won't take my eyes off him. Don't worry about anything here, just take care of getting Cyndi back."

Glen went to his office to arrange to leave for the day. He told Ron Ridgway, his business partner, about Cyndi, and Ron suggested he call the religion editor of the *Atlanta Journal-Constitution*. Ron vaguely remembered seeing an article about the Children of God in the paper some time back, and suggested that they might be able to give us some information about the group. He also offered to go with us to Tennessee.

Glen called the newspaper. The religion editor was very concerned about our daughter, and told us what she knew about the Children of God. She promised to have someone call us who knew a lot more about the group than she did. Unfortunately, she said, she couldn't give out the number. This really sounded strange to me. It sounded like the lady was afraid of the Children of God.

A short time later, Glen got a call from a Mrs. Gaines whose son had been involved in the group for a brief time eighteen months earlier. She told Glen about her son's involvement, and said it had taken him a year to get over the effects of being with the group.

She gave Glen a lot of information, and I was alarmed when she told us some of the same things Bo had told us the night before. They were a cult, led by a man named David Berg (who was also known as Moses David or Mo). Members of the Children of God believed that Berg was a prophet, and that his Mo letters were inspired revelation, and equal to the Scriptures. They had renounced the world, their families, and all worldly possessions. The money they collected was sent to Mo except for a small amount to run the colony. She told us of many families who had lost their children to this group, never to see them again. The more I heard, the more alarmed I became.

Glen was given the phone number of a man who had been accused of kidnapping young people out of the cults, and deprogramming them. Glen called the number in California and spoke with his secretary. She was quite guarded on the phone since she didn't know us, but she told Glen that he would not be able to help us, that he was in Denver on trial for kidnapping, as the result of helping another family recover their daughter. She did, however, give him some information about the Children of God.

Glen was sobered by what he heard. He said, "Lee, it is the same story. No matter who I talk to, the same warning. You may never see your daughter again."

Well, I didn't want to hear that again. I didn't want to accept that at all. I thought we'd come across a bunch of alarmists or some sort of lunatic fringe. My mind was spinning: missing kids, deprogrammers, secret phone numbers—I'd never heard of anything like *this!*

Maybe these other kids were just running away from a bad situation and didn't want to be found. Our case was different, I was sure. We were a close-knit Christian family. Cyndi was a bright, sensible girl. She wouldn't get involved in a cult! She knew better!

We had been given the phone number of Rev. Craven, a

Presbyterian minister in Chattanooga, but we were unable to reach him before we left Atlanta. We decided to go to Chattanooga, not knowing what we would do when we got there, but we felt reassured by the Lord this was the right thing to do. About halfway to Chattanooga we stopped at a pay phone, and Glen reached Rev. Craven at his office. He was very cordial and told us to come to the church when we arrived in town, and meanwhile, he would do his best to locate the commune.

We drove on in silence, all of us deep in our own thoughts. I was glad Ron had offered to go with us. He was calm and unruffled, and it was nice having a friend along.

I laid my head back on the car seat, watching the scenery change as we drove. We were coming out of the foothills now, into the more mountainous regions of north Georgia. This was my favorite part of the ride from Atlanta to Chattanooga. From the road we could see beautiful rock formations, sharp cliffs and waterfalls.

We followed a long curve in the highway, a high cliff blocking our view. Suddenly, the cliff gave way to a breathtaking view of a valley and beyond it the mountains of Tennessee. Somewhere out there, in those distant mountains, was our daughter. How could we find her in such a vast area? She could be anywhere. I knew I should be worried and scared, but I felt so peaceful. It was as if the hand of the Lord was lifting us and guiding us. I was concerned, but not fearful.

As the miles rolled by, my mind went back over the years and I thought about Cyndi's childhood. She had always been such a happy girl. Everyone liked her. She seemed to bring the sunshine with her. Could this girl angrily leave her family and friends, and join a cult? I couldn't get this question out of my mind.

We arrived in Chattanooga and went straight to the Presbyterian church, where Rev. Craven welcomed us. He was a handsome, dynamic man with a pleasant, direct manner. He told us he had cancelled his appointments for that day to meet with us. After Glen's phone call, he had called the police and the FBI but they had been unable as yet to locate the colony. He had talked to school officials and had called Cyndi's place of employment. She had quit her job without proper notice, he told us, having simply called her boss to tell him she wouldn't be back.

Rev. Craven told us that a family in his church had a son who had been taken by the Children of God in Atlanta, and that he had helped to get him out. His information was the same as we had heard earlier. He told us the boy had to undergo extensive psychiatric treatment, and that after a year he was able to return to engineering school.

"After a year!" I said.

"Yes, it seems to take about a year for these kids to get back on their feet, even after just a few days in the cult."

He told us that if we found Cyndi, her name would be changed, and that she would no longer consider us her family. She would have renounced her American citizenship, signed over her power of attorney, and forsaken all her worldly possessions. Glen and Ron and I just sat there for a few minutes trying to let all this sink in.

Rev. Craven seemed to sense we were having a hard time with this. He had worked with many families since his first experience and he knew what we were feeling. He told us he didn't know quite what to do now, and he suggested we have a word of prayer.

Just as he said "Amen" the phone rang. It was his foster daughter. She asked him if he was still looking for the Children of God commune. He said, "Yes, do you know where it is?"

She said yes. That day, while she was in town, some members of the cult had stopped her on the street and had given her a tract. Since she knew her foster father needed information about their commune, she talked to them. They seemed pleased by her interest, and they invited her to come to a Bible study at the commune that night.

Rev. Craven said, "Praise the Lord!" and wrote down the

address. He told her he loved her, hung up, and dialed the police.

This was fantastic! We had only been in town for half an hour, and here we were with the address of the commune that police and FBI couldn't find. God was really moving fast.

Chapter 4

With all the stories I had been told that day of brainwashing, and hypnotism, and spiriting children away in the night, I guess I expected to meet a bunch of wild-eyed cultists, living in seclusion behind drawn drapes on a deserted farm. What we did find was probably harder to deal with.

We called the police and asked a patrol car to accompany us. We followed it for what seemed like an endless drive. We drove to the far edge of the city limits, through suburbs, and up into the hills where the houses seemed to be nestled into the side of the mountains. Finally, we came to a neighborhood of neat duplexes and found the address at the end of a cul-de-sac. We'd been told that kids were taken out the back way if parents appeared at the front door. So Rev. Craven, the policeman, and I went to the front door, and Ron and Glen went around the back.

A young man in his early twenties opened the door and asked, "Hello, can I help you?" He was dressed in jeans and a casual shirt. Several small children were trying to push past him to see who was at the door. A little girl was holding a stuffed lion that I recognized to be Cyndi's.

"What's your name?" the policeman asked him.

"Obadiah" the young man said. He was about six feet tall and very thin, with brown hair, which he wore rather long, and glasses. He looked pale, as if he didn't get outdoors very much.

"Is Obadiah your real name?" Rev. Craven asked.

"It's more real than the one my parents gave me," he said, looking Rev. Craven in the eye.

"Let's have the one your parents gave you," the policeman said.

Obadiah gave him his real name, and the policeman wrote it down.

"Who rents this apartment?" the policeman asked.

"It's in my name," Obadiah answered. "What's this all about?"

"Do you know a girl named Cyndi, or anyone who's ever been named Cyndi?"

"Yes, sir," he answered, "but she's not here right now."

"Where is she?" I asked.

"Why are you looking for her? Is she in some kind of trouble or something?"

"No," the policeman said. "Her parents are trying to locate her, and we understand she's moved in here with you. Is that right?"

"Yes, sir, she's joined our ministry and will be serving God one hundred percent."

"I'm Cyndi's mother," I said. "May I come in and talk to you? We'd like to know more about your ministry."

Glen and Ron came to the door then, and we all introduced ourselves to Obadiah. He stepped back and invited us in.

The commune was a two-story duplex with a living room, kitchen, and powder room on the first floor, and the bedrooms upstairs. It was clean and sparsely furnished. My sewing machine was the only piece of furniture in the living room.

Obadiah told us that Cyndi had decided to forsake the world, and join their commune. Now she was out with some of the elders, and he didn't know when she would be back. I asked him if I could see her room. He readily agreed, and led me upstairs.

Cyndi obviously had the most possessions in the colony. The other bedrooms contained only sleeping bags, and a few personal toiletries. There were no books or pictures and trinkets like most college kids have. Cyndi's room, however, was filled with school books, family pictures, posters, several Bibles, luggage, and small appliances. The closet was full of clothes.

The little girl with the stuffed lion told me that Cyndi had forsaken her clothes to her mother, and that all these "worldly" things were going to be given away.

We talked with Obadiah and asked him questions about the colony and asked what their beliefs were. He gave us some Mo letters. The one he gave us first was called *You've Gotta Be a Baby*. It looked like a miniature comic book with a big baby in a diaper on the front. It was simple, scriptural, and without apparent error. It could have been something we would expect our younger children to get in Sunday school or Bible school. Everything looked very innocent. Could these people really be as bad as we had been told? They didn't look sinister to me at all. I decided to ask Obadiah about the ministry, and about his personal beliefs. Perhaps Rev. Craven was wrong about these people.

"Tell me about the Children of God," I said. "I've been hearing some really negative things about the group, but I want to find out about it for myself."

"That sure is an unusual attitude for a parent," he said. "If more parents would come to us and ask about it, there would be a lot less misunderstanding about our ministry."

With that, Obadiah went into the story of how the group was founded, and he told us of their desire to leave the materialism of the world, and serve God one hundred percent.

Rev. Craven asked Obadiah some questions, and Obadiah became very agitated. He obviously did not like Rev. Craven, and I couldn't understand that. Then I saw the reason.

"You don't approve of anyone in the ministry in the organized churches, do you?" he asked Obadiah.

"No, sir," he said. "The seminaries of today are run by Satan himself. Man can learn about the Bible just by reading it. God ordains ministers, not schools."

21

They had a short discussion about this, both quoting Scripture to prove their point

I tried to get off the subject of seminaries, and back to what the ministry of the Children of God was really all about.

"What is your personal relationship to Jesus Christ?" I asked him.

"Jesus is the Son of God, the Messiah. Believing in Him is the only way to have eternal life." Then he quoted John 3:16: "For God so loved the world, that he gave his only begotten Son, that whosoever believeth in him should not perish, but have everlasting life."

"Have you accepted Him as your Savior, or only acknowledged that He is the Savior of the world?" I asked.

"I've accepted Him personally," he said.

The phone rang, and Obadiah left the room to answer it. When he came back, his attitude was completely changed. He seemed to be hostile and impatient with us.

"I'm going to have to ask you people to wait outside," he said. "I have a lot of work to do, and I need to get these children down for their naps."

We wondered if the phone call had anything to do with Cyndi. Could Bo have found her and given them some trouble? All kinds of thoughts raced through my mind.

We left the house, telling the policeman that we would sit in our car and wait for Cyndi to return. We thanked him for coming with us, and he left.

We sat in our car talking to Rev. Craven for about an hour or so. The sun was beating down, and the temperature was near a hundred degrees. We were very uncomfortable in the heat, and we were all getting restless. We wondered why Cyndi didn't come back.

"Maybe she's not coming back at all," Glen said. "Maybe that guy is just stalling, and they're just waiting for us to leave. Do you think Obadiah called somewhere and told them not to bring Cyndi back here?"

"That's possible," Rev. Craven said. "I think we should take

22

the offensive, and stir this place up a little."

"What do you mean?" I asked.

"You said that's your sewing machine in there, right?"

"That's right," I said. "Cyndi borrowed it to make some clothes for school this fall."

"I think we should go to the door and insist that Obadiah give it to you. If we get persistent, he'll call the police. It may be just what we need to get some publicity about the group. Our statements would be taken for the newspapers, and at least it may start some people thinking. It would bring the cult to the public's attention, and make the address of the commune public."

Glen and I looked at each other. "What do you think?" I asked.

"I don't know. I do want to get Cyndi away from them. At this point, I'm willing to try anything."

"I really don't give two hoots about that old sewing machine, or anything else in there, for that matter. What I want is Cyndi."

We went to the door, and Glen said, "Have you heard anything about Cyndi yet? Do you know when she'll be coming back?"

"No," Obadiah said. "I don't know if she'll even be back today at all. She may be staying somewhere else for the next few days. If the Lord has led the elders to minister to someone, they may be gone for a while. Maybe even as long as a week."

"In that case," Glen said, "I'd like to take the sewing machine home with us. You wouldn't mind, would you?" Glen walked across the room and picked up the sewing machine.

"Please put that down," Obadiah said, his face flushing. "If you don't put it down, I'll call the police."

Glen continued to carry the sewing machine toward the door.

"I'm going to call the police," Obadiah said, and he walked back into the kitchen. We could hear him talking to someone on the phone. Glen had put the sewing machine in the car and had returned to the house by the time Obadiah was finished with his phone call.

Rev. Craven said, "May I use your phone? I'd like to call the newspapers. This would make a great story. I can see it now," he said, running his finger in the air under an imaginary headline, "MOTHER JAILED FOR TAKING SEWING MACHINE FROM CULT COMMUNE. We could get a picture of this lady, too. Everyone can see she's the criminal type."

Rev. Craven looked as if he were enjoying himself, but I wasn't. I wondered what in the world I was doing here, and how this crazy day would end.

Obadiah said we could not use the phone, and he asked us to leave.

Glen said, "I'm sick of all this fooling around. I'm just going to take all of Cyndi's things. Let's get her stuff in the car." He walked up the stairs, strode into her room, grabbed clothes and books by the armful and took them out to the car. The rest of us helped him.

I was shaking like a leaf. The police were coming, and we were taking her stuff, and we didn't know where our daughter was. I was sure we were doing something illegal.

Rev. Craven and Glen looked like they were sure this was the right thing to do, so I just kept putting things in the car.

Out at the car, Rev. Craven said, "These people are just as interested in Cyndi's things as they are in her. We can use her possessions to get them to produce her, if they know where she is."

I looked at Ron to see how he was reacting to all of this. He looked hot and tired, but I couldn't tell what was going on in his head.

"What do you think about all this, Ron?" I asked.

"I think it's a mess," he said.

Well, he had that right, but that still didn't tell me what he thought.

The police car drove up just as we were putting the last of her things in the car. A burly policeman got out of the car, and Obadiah came out of the house and locked the door behind him from the outside. He walked across the yard, and talked to the policeman, pointing to us, and gesturing as he spoke. We just stayed where we were, leaning on the car.

The policeman came over to us, and asked us if we had taken these things without the permission of the person whose house they were in.

"Yes, we did," Glen said. "I'm responsible for it."

"There's a law against that sort of thing," the policeman drawled.

"These things belong to my daughter, and some of them are mine."

"I have no way of knowing that, now do I?" the policeman asked.

"I guess not," Glen said, "but you might ask that young man if they belong to him or our daughter."

"Just whose things are these." he asked Obadiah.

"They belong to the colony."

"Who gave them to the colony?"

"Their daughter."

"Just exactly where is the young lady in question?" he asked all of us.

Everyone said they didn't know. The policeman asked all of us when we had seen her last, took our names and addresses, and Cyndi's full name and address, and wrote everything down in his little black book.

"What's this all about, anyway?" he asked. "What's the problem here?"

I told him of the phone call we got in the middle of the night, and told him we just wanted to talk to our daughter and find out what was going on. Rev. Craven told him that this group of people took kids away and kept them from their parents, and brainwashed them, and most kids need psychiatric help when they get away from the group.

The policeman looked at Rev. Craven as if he were mad.

"I see," he said dryly. He shook his head. "I don't understand you religious people fighting over kids." Pointing a stubby finger at us he said, "Now what I want you people to do is take all that stuff out of your car, and put it back into that house, including the things you say are yours. If you don't, I'm going to run all of you in."

We all looked at Glen to see what he was going to do. I could tell he was furious with the policeman. I hoped he would be cool and not rile this cranky police officer any further.

I took Glen by the arm, and walked a few feet away from the rest of them. "The Bible says to obey the law, Glen, and I think the Lord would want us to put that stuff back."

"You're right," he said. "Besides, if we're sitting down there in jail, we might miss Cyndi if she comes back here."

We walked back to the group, and Glen said, "We'll put the stuff back. It's not these things we want anyway, it's our daughter."

We put the things back in the living room, after Obadiah indicated that's where he wanted them, and we returned to our car to wait for Cyndi.

It was too hot inside the car, so we stood around it, or sat on the curb. We were all hot and tired and thirsty. My head was starting to hurt, and I was getting sunburned.

The policeman came over to where we were leaning on our car, and asked us how old Cyndi was.

"Eighteen," I answered.

"Well, she's of legal age," he said grandly. "You have no business meddling in her life, anyway. You couldn't tell her what to do even if she does come back here. I think I'll just stick around and see that nobody's rights are violated."

I had never met such an obnoxious man in my life. He stood there, lecturing us on Cyndi's rights as an eighteen-year-old, repeating the same things over and over, as if we were too dense to get it the first two or three times. We all knew there was no point in discussing it with him, so we just let him go on and on like a broken record.

Finally, Rev. Craven said, "I'm going to ask one of the neighbors if I can use their phone." He pointed to a house on one side of the commune.

I wanted to call Bo too, so I started to go with him, but I said, "Would you mind if we go there?" I pointed to the house on the other side of the colony. I wondered why I had said that, but I was soon to see it was the Lord providing for us again.

There was a wonderful Christian family living there. We told them about our problem briefly, and asked if we could use their phone. They let us use the phone, gave us cold drinks, and prayed with us. The Lord was providing for us at every turn.

We called Bo's house from our new-found haven, and Bo had just returned—WITH CYNDI!

Chapter 5

Excitedly we asked him how he had found her. He told us he had been driving the streets of Cleveland looking for her, thinking she might be out witnessing with other members of the commune. He had spotted her handing out literature with two men in a shopping mall parking lot. He got out, hugged her, and still holding onto her said, "Come for a ride with me. I want to talk to you." The elders told her she couldn't go, so Bo pushed her in the van, and took off with her. He said she was really mad, and she told him he was kidnapping her.

He told us on the phone, "They've really done a job on her. She's so spaced out she doesn't even know what day it is. She seems to have lost about four or five days."

Rev. Craven got on the phone, and told Bo who he was and where we were. He told Bo to bring Cyndi to the commune so she could take her things, and think over her decision for a few days. He gave Bo directions, and told him we would be waiting there for him and Cyndi.

We were outside standing near the car when Bo's van pulled up about an hour later. I was not prepared for the sight I saw. Bo told us on the phone that Cyndi was in bad shape, but I didn't realize just how bad till I saw her.

She stumbled getting out of the van, and seemed to be having a hard time keeping her balance. We started toward her, and she hesitated, as if she were trying to get her bearings. She was wearing an old shirt of her father's over a pair of jeans.

She had on a pair of wooden-soled sandals that clacked on the pavement as she walked toward us. As she came closer, I could hardly believe the condition she was in. Her hair was a tangled mess and looked as if it had not been combed in days. She looked tired, dirty, and disheveled. Her face was flushed, and her eyes had a strange glassy look. It was almost like someone had drained out the real Cyndi, and this was all that was left. For the first time, real fear gripped me, and I knew in my heart that Cyndi had been seriously affected.

She raised her hand and with a grand gesture, that included Bo, Obadiah, the policeman, Glen, Ron and I, said, "I love all of you." She held out her hand toward Obadiah, and said, "I love my new family," and turning toward us, she said, "I love my former family." Her hand was trembling, and she seemed to be struggling to keep her thoughts and words clear. Glen went to her and put his arms around her.

"I love you too, Cyndi," he said. "How about a hug for dad?"

She hugged him and stepped back away from him quickly. "I have to tell you all something," she said. "I've found a new and better way to serve the Lord, and I want to tell you about it."

I went to her and hugged her and told her I loved her. She returned my embrace then backed away from me, like she had her father. She seemed annoyed.

"You all are making such a big deal out of this, coming up here and everything. I'm eighteen, and I can handle my own life now. I don't want anyone telling me what to do with my life."

"I see that you're angry," I said.

"Yes, I'm angry. Bo kidnapped me! He had no right to rip me off like that!"

I had never known her to be mad at Bo before, and I was surprised at the intense anger I saw in her. She seemed suddenly to be angry at everyone.

"I'd like to hear about your new commitment," I said.

She turned her head away from me and coughed. She obviously had a bad cold. She looked very sick to me. Her voice

30

was lower than usual, and she was talking so differently that it scared me.

I touched her forehead. It was hot. This was not just the heat from a sweltering July afternoon, but a fever.

"You're sick, Cyndi. Have you had this cold long? You should see a doctor," I said.

Irritably she brushed my hand away. "I don't believe in doctors and medicine any more. Being sick is of the devil. Satan just tries to bring sickness on us to disrupt our witnessing. I'm tired of this corrupt systemite world. I'm not going back to that systemite school, or job, or to your materialistic suburbia!"

"What are you going to do? Do you want to stay here at the commune?"

"I don't know. I'm all confused." She looked like she might cry.

Glen said, "Of course she's not staying here." Looking firmly at me, he said, "Don't even give her such a choice!"

Rev. Craven came over and introduced himself to her. "I've heard a lot of nice things about you from your parents, Cyndi. They love you, and they just want to be sure you're making this decision with a clear head."

Cyndi shook his extended hand, and said, "I appreciate everyone's concern, but I can handle my own life."

"I'm sure you can," Rev. Craven said, "but how about telling your folks about your decision, so they won't be worried? Wouldn't you like them to be behind you in whatever you do with your life? They just want to know what's happening with you because they love you." Cyndi was coughing again, and she looked tired and sick.

"I want them to know what I'm doing and why. I wrote them a letter telling them all about it. There was no need for them to come all the way up here."

"Well, now that they are here, how about sitting down with them somewhere and telling them all about it?"

"I—don't know." She seemed to be confused, struggling to make a decision.

31

Obadiah, who had not said anything since Cyndi arrived, said, "She's doesn't have to explain anything to anyone. She's of age, and she can't be coerced by anyone to leave here." Looking Cyndi in the eye, he said, "You remember that, Cyndi. No one can force you to leave here. The policeman here will see to it that no one forces you to go against your will either."

Glen's face was white now, in spite of the heat. The tension of the long ordeal was beginning to show. My normally cool, collected husband was mad! He clenched his fists, and started toward Obadiah. I stepped in front of Glen, putting my arms around him. Ron moved quickly to his side, and put a restraining hand on his arm.

With my arms firmly around him, I said, "It would be foolish to hit Obadiah. We're supposed to be the good guys, remember? Besides, I'm the hothead in this family." I thought joking about the situation would make Glen back off. The policeman had come over to Cyndi now, and he was asking her about her meeting with the Children of God.

"You're going to have to make up your mind what you're going to do," he said. "I don't have all day to stand around here. I personally don't care what you do, but make up your mind. I should have been off duty a long time ago."

Pastor Craven said, "Why don't we go to the church and sit down and talk this over. I'd like to share some things with you, and I'm sure your parents want to know how you feel about things, so they can know best how to help and support you."

"I'm so tired," she sighed. "I'll go with you to the church. Bo told me a bunch of stuff about the Children of God, and now I'm confused."

Obadiah said, "Just remember, God is not the author of confusion. Remember when your confusion started."

Glen glared at Obadiah, and he backed away.

"Get your things," Glen said. "You're going with us right now."

"Okay," she said. "I'll go with you."

"Are you leaving with them of your own free will?" the policeman asked.

"Yes," she said. "My parents won't do anything to hurt me."

Obadiah came over to her and said, "I see the hard situation you have here. Don't worry about anything. No matter how this turns out, we'll be in touch with you. We won't forsake you. Remember what we've taught you." We put her things in Bo's van as quickly as we could get them in.

I hugged Bo, and thanked him for his help. He looked so tired.

"Isn't this exam week?" I asked.

"Yes, and I have my Greek exam in the morning."

"You'd better not come with us to the church. I know you'll need to study, and get some sleep."

"Okay," he said. "I'll go on back to my place now, but I'll come down to Atlanta next weekend, and bring all of Cyndi's stuff then."

Bo took Cyndi by the arm, and led her away from the rest of us where they talked privately for a minute or two. He kissed her good-bye, and told all of us he'd see us in a few days.

We went to the church where Rev. Craven's lovely wife brought us some coffee. We visited for a while, just relaxing and enjoying the cool pleasant comfort of the church parlor.

Pastor Craven did most of the talking and shared with Cyndi about his experience with the boy in his church who was involved in the Children of God. He told her that the cult was a subversive, pro-Communist political group, that they had never gotten anyone off drugs as they claimed, and that all contributions for "foreign missions" went directly to David Berg in Switzerland.

He had a wealth of information, and Cyndi listened politely. She seemed to like Rev. Craven and was able to carry on a conversation with him, but it was still in that strange, remote way.

We talked a long time with the Cravens, sometimes about the Children of God, and sometimes about other things. Rev.

Craven asked Cyndi about herself, her studies, her interests, and her relationship with Christ.

She responded, but didn't seem to want to talk about her past too much. She seemed to get confused or tired when he touched on brothers and sisters or her family life.

She told him she was saved, that she had given her life to Christ when she was twelve years old. That hadn't changed, she said, and never would. However, she was disillusioned with organized churches. She said she felt they had strayed away from the truth. She resented the legalism she found in school. She had come in contact with some girls from small country churches who had criticized her and others for wearing jeans, having pierced ears, and wearing make-up of any kind.

We pointed out to her these people were in a vast minority and that there would always be this kind of people around. They were like the Pharisees of Jesus' day.

She told us that you didn't find this sort of thing in the commune. Everyone was accepted just as they were, and that love abounded, and all were welcomed and none were judged. She also told us she was sick of the way the country was being run and that it was time for a revolution! People were being oppressed and nothing was being shared. She rattled off statistics, and accusations against America and democracy in general.

We were speechless. Glen and I just looked at each other while Rev. Craven fielded these questions and accusations. Ron sat silent. Cyndi had been raised in a very patriotic home. What had happened to her in just five days? She was anti-American, against organized church, and just generally hostile toward anything that was part of the "system."

Rev. Craven asked her how she felt about higher education. "I'm not sure," she said. He told her he knew the Children of God's stand was that all education was of the devil. She said that she knew that, but she couldn't agree with them on that point. She loved school, and she couldn't let them get rid of her books. She had forsaken them, but she still had them, she said.

34

He asked her, "Did you forsake everything?"

"Everything but this," she said. She touched her shawl. I had crocheted it for her and she had been holding it since we came from the commune. "I couldn't forsake this. My mother made it for me."

"How did the commune's shepherd feel about your keeping something of your own?" Rev. Craven asked.

"He told me that as I matured as a Christian I would give it up. I don't want to give this up, though. This is the only thing I really can't forsake."

I looked at my pretty, bright daughter sitting there spouting pro-Communist propaganda and I wondered what they had done to her.

Through Rev. Craven's questioning, we learned that she had renounced her American citizenship and had signed over her power of attorney to the shepherd.

It was getting late, and I turned the conversation to what Cyndi's plans were. I could see that she was not able to handle much, so we just talked about the next few days.

She told us she would not go home with us. I asked her where she wanted to go. She said she didn't know.

"Do you want to go back to the apartment?" I asked.

"No."

"Do you want to go back to the commune?" I asked.

Glen flashed me an angry look.

"I'm not sure."

Rev. Craven very generously offered to let her stay with his family for a few days, but she declined that offer too. She just sat there, glassy-eyed, confused, and belligerent, clutching her shawl like a small child clings to a special blanket.

I'd had enough of her indecision, and I was very tired. I said, "Okay Cyndi, your dad and Ron have a business to run, and they have to get back to Atlanta. I'm going to stay with you until your fever is gone, and you've been able to make some decisions about your future."

She said, "No. I don't want you to stay with me. You'll try to influence me to leave the colony for good!" I assured her that we would not even discuss it until she was feeling better.

"No!" she said. She really looked panicky. When had I become the enemy? Cyndi and I were always so close. Now she was upset about me even staying with her for a few days.

Her voice was shaky, her lower lip quivering, and she insisted that I was *not* staying with her. She said she had decided to sleep in Bo's van.

I said, "Fine, I'll sleep there too." Rev. Craven gave me the thumbs up sign behind her, indicating that my tenacity was the way to go.

She said, "I may go back to the Children of God."

"Fine," I said. "If they're the sweet, open-minded Christians that you describe, they'll welcome a systemite like me."

The thought of me sleeping at the commune seemed to tickle her.

She slumped back in her chair and smiled "Okay, you win. I'll go to Atlanta with you, but I'm not staying at home. I'll stay with one of my girl friends."

She couldn't seem to figure out just which girl friend. As I mentioned names, she always had a reason why she couldn't stay with that one. I breathed a little prayer and asked the Lord to give us wisdom and patience.

I finally said, "How about Gail Crow?" Gail was one of my closest friends, but she was also Cyndi's friend. Gail was a sharp gal, and the kids all loved her. For the first time all day Cyndi agreed with what I suggested.

I excused myself to make the call to Gail to see if she could take Cyndi for a few days. There was no answer. It was after 10:00 P.M. and I knew that Gail wouldn't keep her little girl out much later than that, even in the summer. I decided I'd call back again. A few minutes later I did so and Gail answered. I told her very briefly what had happened and that Cyndi had agreed to stay with her if it was convenient. She said of course Cyndi could come.

"You know this is really weird," Gail said. "I had gone to bed early, and had pulled the phone out of the jack and was sound asleep. I woke up with a strong urge to plug in the phone, but I ignored it, and turned over and tried to go back to sleep. I couldn't get rid of the feeling that I should plug in the phone. So I plugged it in, it rang and it was you." She laughed. "Have you all been praying?"

"Have we been praying!" I told her we'd be there about two in the morning or so. "Just come on," she said, "whatever the time." Praise the Lord for Christian friends!

If anyone could get Cyndi's head on straight, it would be Gail.

Chapter 6

The four of us headed back to Atlanta, not knowing what lay ahead, or how long it would take for Cyndi to get over her five days with the Children of God.

On the way home, Cyndi was hostile and she made it very clear that she was not at all happy about coming with us. She went on and on about politics in America and corruption in high places. America was falling, she said, a new better socialistic government would take over, there would be equality for all. Glen was irritated with her, and they got into a couple of arguments. I suggested we not talk about politics until later.

We rode in silence for a long time, then Cyndi sat up straight and said, "You wouldn't get a deprogrammer or anything like that would you?"

"A deprogrammer!" I said. "Of course not!" She seemed scared and asked us several times if we were going to trick her, and take her to a deprogrammer. We assured her that we would not, and she relaxed a little.

She told us of stories she heard at the colony of kids being "ripped off" (a new phrase she used frequently) by their parents and placed in the hands of a deprogrammer, who strapped or tied them down, and deprived them of food and sleep. She said these kids had been slapped, had pillows held over their faces, and finally, when broken, would deny Christ, and forsake the Children of God and their new "family." Members were instructed to do everything in their power to keep from being deprogrammed. All of them were told that deprogrammers were demon-possessed.

I said, "Cyndi, do you think that your father and I would ever do anything so terrible to you? We love you Cyndi, and we'd never intentionally hurt you. Have we ever?"

After a pause she said, "No."

I had seen a movie on television a few years earlier about a deprogrammer. He was working for a father trying to get his daughter out of a commune. I recalled that she was kidnapped, taken to a motel room, and handled in much the same way Cyndi had described. No, we surely wouldn't get a deprogrammer for Cyndi.

We arrived at Gail's house at about three in the morning and Gail got up and welcomed us. Glen and I filled Gail in very briefly on what had happened, and we left.

Cyndi had told us not to call over there and "bug her." She'd call us when she had thought things through for herself.

Gail called me about noon the next day, and said Cyndi had slept until then, and that she had a fever, and perhaps should see a doctor.

I talked briefly with Cyndi, and she said, "No doctor. I'll be fine."

The next morning the phone rang. It was Cyndi.

"Mom, come and get me!" she cried. "The devil is going to get me! My thoughts come flying out of my head. I can't control them, please come for me, mom!" She was hysterical.

I said, "I'll be right there. Where's Gail?"

"She's gone. Hurry, mom!"

My thoughts were racing. I hoped that Gail had taken her daughter with her. "Cyndi, where's Kim? Did she go with her mother?"

"No, she's here."

"Oh my Lord, Cyndi! Think! Is she in the pool?"

"No, no. Hurry, mom!" She was crying, and babbling about seeing her thoughts leaving her head.

I raced over there as fast as I could, praying that I wouldn't be stopped for speeding. Then I realized I should have called Glen. What would I do with Cyndi when I got there?

When I arrived, Gail was already home, and had calmed Cyndi down. They were talking. Cyndi felt that she was losing her mind. Gail explained to her that people who are losing their minds don't rationally talk about it and ask for help. The three of us talked for a few minutes, and then Cyndi and I left.

We arrived home and I got her settled in her old room. She seemed very remote and emotionless. I thought this strange in light of the very emotional outburst at Gail's house. Even more strange, she was not at all friendly to her brother and sisters. She just stayed in her room. The other children didn't know how to respond to her or what to think of her behavior. Neither did I, but I decided to leave her alone until she got her thoughts collected and wanted to talk.

I was working in the kitchen when I heard her come in. I turned around and she was standing by the refrigerator, her eyes wide. She had the most horrible, frightened look on her face. She seemed almost unable to get the words out.

"Mom, help me." It was almost a whisper.

"What's the matter, honey?"

"I don't know! I'm so scared. I keep thinking that I'm going to kill myself! Horrible thoughts are coming to me. I'm so afraid. When I try to think, and figure everything out, my thoughts leave my head, and I see them spinning around the room. Do you know what I mean?"

Well, I didn't know what she meant, but I could only try to reassure her and comfort her. I called Glen and he came right home. Cyndi was crying again, and trying to explain what was happening to her to her father. She wanted to know if we could see them as they were leaving her. We told her that we could not and that no one could see another person's thoughts. She was getting more upset by the minute. She began to pace back and forth in the kitchen and family room. Nothing she said made much sense, and I thought she must be having a nervous breakdown.

41

Glen said, "Cyndi, would you be willing to see a doctor? I really think you need help."

"I know I need something, or someone, to help me."

Glen called a psychiatrist and made arrangements to have Cyndi examined as an outpatient. At the hospital the doctor determined that she had bronchitis, was severely disoriented, and was hallucinating. He recommended that she sign herself into the hospital for a few days. She was willing, and spent the next three days in the mental health ward.

The doctor told us when he discharged her, that she was reacting as if she had been given a large dose of a drug. That could have caused the hallucinations. He said he felt that Cyndi would be fine. She had no serious problems, or mental disorder, but needed rest.

Cyndi returned home, but she was far from "fine." Her personality and disposition were not at all as they had been for eighteen years.

After resting quietly at home for several days, we talked with her about the doctor's opinion that she had been drugged. She became very angry. "Those people don't use drugs! They don't give other people drugs either!"

I said, "Well, how do you account for your hallucinations?"

"I don't know."

"Cyndi, I'd like to talk to you about the Children of God. Will you tell me about them? I haven't wanted to talk to you about it before, because you were so upset, but I really do have some questions."

"Okay," she said. "I'll talk about it today, but not after that. Ask your questions."

"How did you meet them?"

"They were handing out literature on the corner, and when I was walking home from work, they talked to me and gave me some of their tracts. I thought they were really interesting. They told me how they lived in a commune, and had forsaken the world, and were following Jesus like the apostles in the New Testament church."

"Did you go with them then?"

"No, we just talked then, and they asked me where I lived, and if I was a Christian. We just had a real nice time talking. They seemed to have it all together more than anyone I had ever talked to before. Later that night they came over to my apartment and we talked a long time. The next day after work they were waiting for me and they gave me a ride home. They asked me to come to the colony for a Bible study and a party."

"What happened then?"

"Well, I went to Chattanooga with them. We had a party and a Bible study, and they told me more about the movement and their leader."

"What did you think of the other people you met there?"

"I was really impressed with all of them. They were so open and loving, and had such joy. I had never seen so many happy faces. They had such love!"

"Did you feel that you needed love?" I asked.

"I hadn't thought about it, but they made my life seem so ordinary by comparison. I was drawn to them because of their loving, happy spirits. Everything was super happy and so positive. Before I knew it, it was two in the morning. They asked me if I wanted to spend the night, since it was such a long way back to Cleveland. I agreed and spent the night at the colony. The next day I didn't have to go to work, and they asked me to go on a picnic with them. I spent the day with them, and we had a real good time."

"When did you decide to leave your apartment and go with them full time?"

"I—don't know. It seems like a dream. I don't know when I decided. I was just there."

"When did you bring your clothes and things from your apartment?"

"I don't remember."

"Don't you remember packing and moving there?" I was amazed that she could remember so little about her move.

"No, I don't remember packing, or even deciding to go with

43

them. I thought that they were interesting and fantastic Christians, but I was just visiting them."

"Are you telling me that you didn't pack your own clothes, and that you never decided to move in with them? If that's the case, do you realize you were kidnapped?"

"Now wait a minute," Cyndi said. "I was not kidnapped. I went with them of my own free will."

"Then why can't you remember packing or deciding to go to live with them?"

"I don't know. I'm all confused."

"When did you realize that you had moved in with them?"

"I don't know."

"What did you think when your clothes suddenly appeared at the colony?"

"I told you, I can't remember! It just all seemed right at the time. Everything seemed right. There was no time, no outside world, just the colony, and the 'family.' "

I asked her, "Did you think of your dad and I and your family here? Didn't you think that we would be worried about you? What about your job and your friends? What about Bo?"

"I did think about it some, but I got confused whenever I thought about anything outside the colony. The others told me that confusion is not of the Lord, and if I get confused when I think about my family and friends, that just proves that they are of the devil. God is not the author of confusion."

"Did that seem logical to you at the time?"

"I guess it did."

"Does that seem reasonable to you now?"

"I don't know. I don't know what is reasonable any more."

"Do you believe that your father and I are of the devil?"

"No, of course not. But a lot of what they told me is true. Our churches and schools are not Christian institutions any longer. Many things have become perverted by Satan."

"Do you believe the Children of God are the only people who have the truth, and are the only group which is right with God?"

She thought this question over for a few moments, and said, "I can't think of any other religious group who has really forsaken all to follow the Lord."

"Then you believe that this is the only true church?"

She said, "The Children of God are a hundred percent committed to Christ. They have forsaken all."

"Do you believe that all Christians should live communally and ask for donations on street corners in order to have a hundred percent commitment?"

Cyndi gave me a disgusted look and said, "I don't know if I would exactly put it that way, but yes I do believe that all Christians should live communally and share everything. That's what the early Christians did."

I was really surprised at her attitude. We had never been a family to feel that we were exclusive in our faith. We had a deep appreciation for all Christian faiths, and were certainly not denominationalists. Although we were members of the Church of God denomination, we were involved in several nondenominational Bible studies, and had recently become involved in the Lutheran Cursillo movement. We were excited about the conversion of several of our friends, and the deepening of the faith of several others after their "Short Course in Christianity."

Cyndi's attitude was not a reflection of her home training. Glen and I knew that our children would be different from us in many respects, but this was pretty far out. I tried to keep the lines of communication open, but it was hard for me to understand her exclusive attitude. She had been active in Campus Crusade for Christ in high school, and she was particularly pleased with their interdenominational position.

I asked her, "What would happen if all Christians decided to live as the Children of God do? If we sold everything, took all the Christian children out of school, quit our jobs, stopped paying taxes, quit the organized churches, and just asked for donations, who would support us? The non-Christian community? Just think about these things."

45

"The disciples left their jobs to follow Jesus," she said.

I said, "The Bible tells us that Jesus was a carpenter. The apostle Paul was a tent maker, and Luke was a doctor. When the disciples were called by Jesus, it was like our modern-day missionaries. I believe that was a special calling. Everyone who is a Christian is not called to the same ministry. It seems that this group is very negative, and is condemning of other Christians. That's not scriptural, Cyndi." After this, Cyndi didn't want to talk any more.

Cyndi decided that she did not want to return to school for the fall quarter. In view of her mental state, her father and I were relieved to have her make that decision.

She took a job in a department store, and we felt she would surely get back to her old self soon. Unfortunately, however, she did not. Where she had always been neat and well-groomed before, she became careless and sloppy in her appearance. She had loved music, and had played the guitar and sang, and belonged to a choir. She now was quiet and withdrawn, and never took her guitar out of its case. Where she formerly had been outgoing and gregarious, she now preferred to be alone. When old friends phoned she would turn down invitations. When they left messages for her to call them back, she would not return the calls.

She seemed to be acting like an undisciplined preteen rather than a girl of nearly nineteen, and she became very difficult to live with.

The psychiatrist noted a very immature attitude and asked me if she had always been immature for her age. I was amazed. I told him that she had always been very mature and very responsible. She could do almost anything she set her mind to. She had always been a big help to me, and had been active at school and at church. The doctor, I felt, found this hard to believe.

Chapter 7

After just a few visits, Cyndi would not return to the doctor. She said that she did not like the "hassle" of going there every week. Glen's clients were some of those hardest hit by the recession. We were feeling the full impact of the economic decline, so we really did not push her to spend sixty dollars a visit for something that she did not feel was helping her.

Mrs. Gaines called to see how Cyndi was doing. I told her that Cyndi had a job, and I was sure that she would be her old self in a short while. She told me of her son's experience with the cult, and warned me that they would try to get in touch with Cyndi, and would try to get her back. She told me of her son being called on the phone by a cult member, and how he felt as if he were being physically drawn into the phone. "Almost like being sucked into the receiver," she said.

Well, I thought that was an incredible story, and I still was not too sure about these people who believed that the new converts were hypnotized and brainwashed. True, Cyndi was not herself, but I really felt at this point that she was just emotionally upset and rebellious.

Mrs. Gaines gave us the telephone number of a young man named David Brubaker, a former Children of God member who had been deprogrammed and who now worked with his deprogrammer, helping other young people get back to reality after their cult experience.

I still didn't like the whole idea of deprogrammers, but Glen

47

felt that he should talk to David. He was very worried about Cyndi and had said several times that it just wasn't like her to act so babyish.

Glen talked to David for a long time on the phone. He said that Cyndi really should be deprogrammed, or she might go back with the group. He also gave Glen the address of the attorney general of the state of New York, and suggested that we send for a report that had been prepared by the Charity Frauds Bureau.

The report stated that the newly recruited members are kept up day and night for many days, and never left alone for a moment. The colony members rotate in shifts so subtly that the unsuspecting "babe" does not even notice that one person slips out and another comes in. They do this very naturally, and keep the new convert up singing, listening to tapes, and reading Mo letters, for an unbearable length of time.

Finally, deprived both of sleep, and of time to think for themselves, the convert's mind is broken. The new "babes" are now ready to accept whatever they are told. A song that is a favorite in the colony is, "You've gotta be a baby." This is also the title of the first tract that the group hands out. The new convert becomes, not a baby, but a non-thinking, order-taking robot. The time varies with the individual, but they are all eventually broken, and the level of maturity is much lower than it was formerly.

Since the organization of the cult in 1969, thousands of teenagers and young adults have abandoned their jobs, school, family, and friends to abruptly join the cult.

In general, Children of God is estimated to have over thirty-five hundred members in sixty-five countries, with more than a hundred and twenty communes in North America and Europe. The young people who are involved seem on the whole, to be the intelligent, middle class, white college student, or young career person.

Directing the lives of the "sheep" is David Brandt Berg, otherwise known as Moses David. The founder and leader of the Children of God, fifty-nine, reportedly lives in Europe, his whereabouts known only to those closest to him.

Through a constant flow of Mo letters, Berg instructs the followers in all aspects of life. The cult members believe the obscenity-laced literature to be the inspired word of God, and that Berg is a modern-day prophet. They believe that Mo letters are a continuation of the Bible for God's chosen few.

Scripture verses, while freely quoted, are used out of context and drastically misinterpreted. Berg, throughout his writings, preaches disdain for the organized church, America, education, the family unit, people holding traditional jobs, and all systemites.

About three hundred and fifty or more Mo letters have been distributed. They deal extensively with such subjects as sex, politics, media manipulation, and the cult's methods of propagation.

The cult has done very well in its distribution of the letters, boasting of a distribution of more than a million pieces of literature a week in 1974. This selling of tracts is called "litnessing" by the Children of God. Litnessing is the full-time occupation of the newly indoctrinated "babes," and they are praised, or scolded in proportion to the amount of money collected.

The average Children of God member earns about fifty dollars a day for two hundred pieces of literature. The more experienced members can earn over a hundred dollars a day and distribute four hundred pieces of literature.

The sales and distributions are recorded nightly, in reports the Children of God members are required to complete. Besides the litnessing results, they are required to list the number of persons they had converted that day. The leaders then prepare what are called "sheep cards." These are the names and addresses of "sheepy" or interested people that the Children of God member has talked to that day. These are followed up with visits, telephone calls, letters, invitations to parties, and Bible studies.

Fifteen percent of the money is kept by the colonies, and the rest is sent to "foreign missions." The group, however, can show no record of mission work, nor is there any evidence of the drug rehabilitation program which, the group says, is a part of their ministry. The money is sent to David Berg, and to date, the Internal Revenue Service cannot locate Berg or his books for examination.

Although the members concentrate on exuding joy and love to the persons they meet on the streets, their primary concern is earning money for their nebulous "causes." They are told when they get money from people that they are ripping off the system and the systemites. They also call it "spoiling Egypt." The only people in whom they have a real interest are those who are possible converts to the cult, or future donors.

The cult members are instructed how to solicit meals from various restaurants. They explain that they are members of a Christian missionary youth organization. They ask if the restaurant manager could help them by donating lunch for two or three of the team. They are very seldom turned down.

The new Children of God members are instructed that parents who will not help support the cause and become donors to the colony are of the devil. Parents are viewed as potential donors, and if they will not submit to the demands for money, their children are not allowed to call or visit them. Many parents keep the money coming in just to keep in touch with their children.

The use by the Children of God of Luke 14:26 and Matthew 10:36, taken out of context, and used in conjunction with Mo letters, can be considered part of a deliberate plan to disrupt familial relationships, the report said.

Prayer meetings aside, only thirty minutes of free time is allotted before lights out. During that time, members are encouraged to correspond with prospective financial supporters and potential Children of God disciples.

Due to rigid scheduling, some of the members were forced to go for days without attending to personal grooming and hygiene. All complaining is considered of the devil and anything short of total contentment and acceptance is considered impious.

Instances of brainwashing and sexual abuse of its members are included in the attorney general's report. One fourteen-year-old girl told investigators that she was repeatedly raped within a Children of God colony. Sarah Berg, the former daughter-in-law of David Berg, testified that prior to her marriage to his son, she was forced by Berg to have sex with her prospective husband in his presence.

There are strict rules forbidding sex before marriage, but the Children of God marriages are sometimes only for a night or two. This varies from one colony to another.

Former members testified that they were in a dream-like state all the while they were in the family, and for some time afterward. They felt like they were walking on a cloud as long as they kept in touch with their key stimuli—prayer, and Mo letters. Psychiatrists say that the cult members are operating in a dream-like state. Their free will is impaired, and they have been altered psychologically.

After understanding more clearly that brainwashing can alter one's personality, and that it does happen in cults, I could understand a little better what Cyndi had been through.

The Patti Hearst case was front page news, with Patti having just been captured by the FBI. My heart ached for her and her family. She had been through such a terrible ordeal. My prayers were that she would be able to regain her former identity, and not be convicted of a crime under the circumstances.

She was later convicted of course, and I could not understand how a person who had been kidnapped, abused, and brainwashed could be found guilty. Though my prayers were with Patti, I think I prayed even more for her mother. I understood the heartache she suffered, and asked the Lord to comfort her, as He had comforted me.

Chapter 8

We had for many weeks respected Cyndi's wishes, and had not talked to her about the Children of God. Now, however, with the information that we had from the attorney general, Glen felt that she should read the report.

She had been very defensive about the group, and we wanted her to see a documented report exposing them for what they really were, a group of people living off the land by begging in the streets; a group intent on the overthrow of our government, paying no taxes, having no outreach ministry, existing totally for the benefit of David Berg and his selected leaders. They were "ripping off" the system with the aid of people handing dimes and nickels to kids soliciting in the streets. We tried to show her that the Mo letters were obviously the writings of a man with a very sick mind.

Cyndi had a hard time reading the report. She would read a few lines, and become very sleepy. Glen would come in from work and ask her, "Did you read the report?" She would tell him that she had read a little, or that she hadn't had time that day. Finally, Glen began reading portions of it to her, and insisting she read to him until they had read it all. He wanted to know what she thought of the report, but she was unable to talk about it very much. She did admit that if it were all true, they were not what she believed them to be.

We were now able to understand a little better what Cyndi had been through, and we tried to be patient and help her get back to normal. We prayed for the restoration of her mind and for her complete healing.

Cyndi had been an accomplished seamstress, and had sewn most of her clothes when she was in high school, so I decided to encourage her to do some sewing for herself. She bought material, but she was unable to cut it out properly. I would finish cutting it for her, then she would make mistakes, and give up and cry.

She seemed so childlike in her behavior that we were really afraid for her. We were glad she wasn't going out much. I wondered how she was managing on her job.

She seemed to need so much sleep, that I encouraged her to go to the doctor for a checkup. She refused.

She also refused to go to church with us, or on any family outings. This is not too unusual for teenagers I realized, but it was unusual for Cyndi to be this distant with us. She was even distant with her little brother Eric, whom she had always adored.

Cyndi seemed to have periods where she had complete lapses of memory. She would drive to the store and not return for hours. When I asked her what took her so long, she'd look surprised, not realizing so much time had passed. "I guess I just sat in the car and thought," she would say.

I finally made an appointment with the doctor and talked with him myself. He told me I couldn't force her to come for help. She also refused to talk to any of our pastors.

Cyndi had a birthday party for Bo at our house, and it was the first time she was able to handle any kind of responsibility since coming home. Bo's parents came, and lots of old friends from high school were invited. They had all gone off to different colleges, so they were always glad to get together again and catch up on the news. Cyndi seemed brighter and more like herself at that party than she had in a long time. My hopes were raised that this was really the end of her depression.

Bo invited Cyndi to go to the mountains with his family over the Labor Day weekend, and I was sure this would cheer her up. She loved the mountains, and she loved Bo's parents and enjoyed being with them. When she got home, I asked her if she had a good time.

"It was okay," she said. That was all.

Bo had transferred to another college in Knoxville, and he invited Cyndi to come up for homecoming. She seemed pleased, but she just didn't have the sparkle and enthusiasm she'd always had before.

Glen and I were a little concerned about her driving all the way to Knoxville by herself, but we realized she had to get back to normal sometime, and we couldn't keep her home with us forever.

She made the trip to Knoxville and back just fine, but she was still distant, and had that strange look in her eyes. We asked her how the weekend went, and she only said, "It was okay." She told us that the girl she stayed with in the dorm was real sweet, and that she met a lot of nice people.

"How's Bo?" I asked.

"He's fine. He likes school."

This was not the same girl who was so much in love with Bo just a week before going with the Children of God.

Cyndi came home from work one afternoon in a strange mood.

I said, "Cyndi, you seem different today, kind of agitated or restless or something. What happened today?"

"Nothing really," she said, "but some people from the Children of God came into the store today."

"Really?" I said, trying to seem unconcerned. "What did they say to you?"

"Nothing much, just that they love me, and that the family really needs me."

"Were these people that you knew from the colony in Chattanooga?"

"No, these were people from Atlanta."

"Did they come there to talk to you, or did they just happen by? What exactly did they say to you?" I wanted to pursue this without letting her sense that I was concerned, but it was difficult.

She said, "Oh, they just showed me some Mo letters, and they asked me if I had ever seen any of these before. I told them I had, and they asked me where. I told them I had been in the family, and knew all about the Children of God. They seemed to know all about me."

That worried me a little, yet here she was at home, and telling me about it, so I guessed that she was finally rejecting their life style.

"What did they say then?"

"They said they knew that I had been in the family, and they knew all about me, and how I had been 'ripped off' by my boy-friend and my parents."

"Do you feel that you were 'ripped off'?"

"Yes, I was ripped off."

"Is that why you're angry with Bo?"

"Yes, I'm angry with Bo. I wanted him to join the family too, but all he could do was put it down."

This was the first time that I had heard that. I could tell that she was angry with Bo, and the rest of the world, for that matter, but she had never verbalized it before.

Cyndi's behavior continued to show radical change. She became hostile and insulting. No one could say a word to her without having a big argument.

Several times she ran to her room, slammed the door, and packed her clothes. We had to talk to her and convince her that she could not move out, that she just was not ready to support herself yet. We told her that we realized she was at an age where she would rather be on her own, and her father suggested that she save some money, and when she was ready financially, and had a roommate, we would help her move. We didn't want her moving out in anger. We tried to convince her that mature people don't just move out with no plan for the future, and nowhere to go. That was like a little child running away from home.

She grudgingly unpacked, but her attitude remained

hostile. If we talked to her about her attitude, she would cry like a young child, and her lip would quiver. We wondered if she were putting us on and we were puzzled and upset.

One day she came home and told me she had been fired from her job. She just couldn't concentrate, she said, and she didn't like "that systemite job" anyway.

Cyndi had held a part-time job all through high school, and had been so well thought of by her employers previously, that this was really a surprise to us. Yet she was different now. We knew that.

Cyndi stayed in bed much of the time for the next few days, and I tried to leave her alone and not bother her. I thought she must be feeling very bad about herself right then.

When she did come downstairs, she was ugly with the family, and she was rude and insulting to everyone that she came in contact with. She seemed to be deliberately starting arguments with me. She insulted my cooking, interfered with my handling of the younger children, and made insulting remarks to me, or about me to the younger children, at every opportunity. The younger children would tell her to "talk nice" to mother. She and Glen had several arguments about her attitude and her insulting remarks to me.

I guessed that she was trying to push me so far that I would ask her to leave. I was determined not to let her get to me. But she *was* getting to me. She had completely disrupted our home. All my energies were being poured out on Cyndi and her problems. I felt that I was neglecting my other children and my husband. I really resented it, too. I was a nervous wreck! I was tired and I was depressed. I was tired of being the long-suffering, understanding good sport. I'd had it!

Cyndi was ruining her life, and I could not understand it. She had a good home, loving parents, above average intelligence, and was beautiful too. She could be and do anything with her God-given assets. How could she just throw away her life like this? She was not turning out to be the kind of person she could be. I didn't really like her as she was. That was shocking to me. I didn't like my own daughter!

I went to my room and got down on my knees and prayed. I really got honest with the Lord, and told Him exactly how I felt about the situation, and about Cyndi. (He knew it anyway). I just poured out my heart to my Father and turned Cyndi over to Him one hundred percent. I had done that before, but then I would think of something that I hadn't tried before, and I would take the situation back and try to work it out myself. Then when I failed in my own human efforts, I would turn her back over to the Lord again. This time, however, she was all His.

Then I took a long objective look at myself. Was my love for Cyndi conditional? Could I only love her if she were obedient, performing the way I thought she should? I didn't like this conversation with myself, but I had to face my feelings squarely. I had to accept her as she was. I knew, in the natural, that I could not do this. I still didn't like this situation, and I asked the Lord to help me love her and accept her no matter what.

I read 1 Corinthians 13, and got myself on the right path. I started by doing loving things for her. I cleaned her room, and did her laundry. I mended a couple of things I knew needed attention. I believed that love never fails. It is the greatest and only lasting spiritual gift.

Cyndi came in a few days later and told Glen and me she would be moving out. She had met some kids who were living in an apartment downtown, and they had asked her to join them.

We reminded her that she had no job, and asked her how she planned to pay for the rent, and her expenses. She said she would be taking a job with one of the girls she would be living with, that we should not try to talk her out of moving, that she had made up her mind, and we should just accept it. We said that we would like to meet her new friends, and she really got nervous.

"No!" she said. "You're always interfering in my business. I want you to get off my back and let me live my own life. Just leave me alone."

She spent the rest of the evening packing her clothes and getting her things together. We just stayed out of her way, and didn't say much to her.

The next morning she was up early. Just after the younger children left for school, she said she was, calling a cab to take her to her new apartment. I offered to drive her, but she refused. It seemed to make her very nervous that I had offered.

Glen usually went to his office early, but this morning he stayed home. He had been listening to our conversation and had heard me offer to drive her.

"Why can't your mother drive you to your new apartment?" he asked.

"I just want to go by myself," she said.

"Why don't you want us to know where you're living?"

"I'll let you know where I'm living after I'm settled. Just don't bug me about it now."

We were perplexed. If she were going to live with someone we knew, we wouldn't be worried. We liked her friends, but these were people we didn't know, and we knew that Cyndi couldn't know them very well either. She would not answer questions about where and when she had met them. She reminded us that she was nineteen now and that she did not have to answer to us about where she was going, or with whom.

She had been very mysterious the last few days, and had been gone a lot. She told us that she had been job hunting, but that she had been unsuccessful. Now, suddenly, she had a job, some new friends, and an apartment. She was right, she was of age, and we could not stop her from leaving.

Glen had to get to work, so there was no more time for discussion. I started to clean up the kitchen, and Cyndi went up to her room to finish packing. A few minutes later, Glen walked into the kitchen. I looked at him in surprise and said, "Did you forget something?"

He said, "Lee, she's going back to the Children of God."

"She wouldn't do that," I said. "She read the attorney

general's report, and she knows what they really are now."

"She's going back with them," he said. He went to the bottom of the stairs and asked Cyndi to come down.

She came downstairs, and said, "What do you want?"

"You're going back with the Children of God aren't you?"

"No," she said, "I'm just going to move in with a bunch of kids in an apartment."

"Are there girls and boys all living together?" Glen asked.

"Why are you asking me all these questions? I don't have to answer to you or anyone else. I'm of age, and I'm going to be on my own from now on."

"I want you to answer me!" Glen shouted.

Cyndi looked pale. Glen seldom raised his voice, but when he did, the children knew they had pushed as far as they could.

"Answer my question," he repeated.

"Yes, there are guys and girls living together in a big house, but the girls live in one part, and the guys live in another part."

"I thought you said it was an apartment."

"It's none of your business if it's a house or an apartment!" she snapped. "Get off my back!"

Glen took her by the arm and shook her. "You watch how you talk to me young lady," he warned. "You're not going anywhere till I get some straight answers from you. Now, just exactly where are you going, and with whom? It's the Children of God, isn't it?"

"Yes!" she shouted. "I'm going back with them. That's the only place I can have peace. I've tried it your way, and I just can't accept your systemite life style. I've been miserable since I've been home. I just can't make it in this kind of life. Everyone wants me to fit into their mold. I feel like I'm being pushed and shoved to fit into your preconceived idea of what I'm supposed to be. Let me be myself! Let me go!"

I was panicky. I said, "Cyndi, would you talk this over with Dr. McLuhan before going?" (Dr. Mac, as we called him, is our associate pastor, and our good friend.)

"No! I will not talk to him, or anyone else. I've made up my

60

mind."

Glen told me to call Dr. Mac anyway. I dialed the church, praying he would not be in a counseling session. I got him on the phone and briefly explained the situation to him. Dr. Mac knew our family well, and he knew Cyndi. He had talked with her on many occasions before. They had always been special friends. Glen had given Dr. Mac the attorney general's report earlier and he knew all about the group.

Dr. Mac said, "Let me talk to her."

I handed the phone to Cyndi and she reluctantly took it from me. She listened for a minute, and then gave Dr. Mac the same kind of answers she had given her father. I was surprised that she would be so rude to him. I heard her say she didn't care what his opinion was, she had made up her mind, and there was nothing more to say about it. She said, yes, she had read the attorney general's report. She had asked the shepherd about it and he had explained to her that it was just a bunch of systemite lies.

She told Dr. Mac that she didn't think much of his church either, and that they were both entitled to their own opinion. With that, she handed the phone back to me.

Dr. Mac said, "Lee , you will have to let her go. She has to learn this lesson the hard way."

I couldn't believe what I heard. Dr. Mac was telling me to let her go, in spite of all he knew about the Children of God. I listened, horrified, as he went on. "I can promise you this, she won't stay with that group."

"What makes you so sure?" I asked.

"She's too smart a girl for that. She knows the Bible better than some of the leaders of the group, who have been fed only with selected verses taken out of context. She'll see through that in no time, and she'll leave. Besides, in the colony, she would be expected to be submissive to the leaders and subject to their every order. You know she's too independent for that group, she's too liberated. She's not going to be submissive to them, or to anyone else right now."

"What if they ship her to another state, and we never see her again?" I asked. "What if she sees through it, and wants to leave, and they won't let her go?" I was crying now. "I don't want to let her go!"

Dr. Mac's voice was kind. "I know it's hard, Lee, but you can't handcuff her to the bedpost. She's a committed Christian, and we'll just have to trust the Lord to take care of her. He can do a much better job of it than we can. Trust Him, and let her go."

I was crying too hard to talk, and I handed the phone to Glen.

Cyndi had returned to her room, and after a few more minutes, Glen finished his conversation with Dr. McLuhan, and hung up.

Glen put his arms around me, and said, "Dr. Mac is right, hon, we have to let her go. She's of age. She's making a bad mistake, but she has to find out for herself." I felt anger at both of these men. They should be doing something, saying something, praying, locking her up, if necessary. But they both said to let her go. I felt they were letting me down.

We went upstairs. Cyndi had all of her things in the hall ready to go. She told us she had called a cab, and would be leaving in a few minutes.

Now I was mad. I said, "If you think that you're taking all this stuff with you, just to forsake it to those people, you've got another think coming. You can take one suitcase of clothes and nothing else."

She put back her record player, her records, her guitar, and several boxes she had packed. She had the most determined, and belligerent attitude I had ever seen. Cyndi had always had a mind of her own, but this was really extreme.

The cab arrived, and she started out the door without her coat. It had turned suddenly and unseasonably cold during the night.

Glen stopped her and said, "Every morning when you wake up, the first thing you'll think will be, 'My father hates the Children of God.'"

62

I got her winter coat out of the closet and put it on her. She turned to me, and put her arms around me, and said, "I love you mother, please don't cry. Thank you for getting my coat."

I held onto her arm, crying. "Cyndi, don't do this, you'll ruin your life. You know, Cyndi, the Bible says that 'you will never see the righteous forsaken, or his seed out begging for bread.' You're choosing a life of begging for a living, and I'm going to stand on the word of God, and trust Him not to permit you to stay with that group of beggars. Please don't go Cyndi, please." I was pleading with her, holding on to her. She pulled away from me, and without looking back, she ran to the waiting cab.

Chapter 9

I turned to Glen, and he put his arms around me. I sobbed uncontrollably for several minutes. We just stood there in the front hall, clinging to each other, unable to speak.

Glen held me close, comforting me as if I were an injured child. He said, "Don't worry hon, she'll be back. She won't last with that group. Trust her to the Lord. She's read the documented proof that the Children of God are not what they claim to be, and she'll come out somehow. I feel sure of it."

I went into the kitchen to get a Kleenex. I wiped my eyes, and looked at Glen. For a man who was talking so confidently, he didn't look too sure of himself. His face looked drawn and worried. I could tell he was just as scared as I was.

"I hope you're right about her coming home," I said.

Glen didn't leave for the office right away. He helped me with the dishes, then we sat in the family room together, not saying much, just holding hands, trying to sort out in our minds what had happened. We were stunned, really shocked by Cyndi's decision to rejoin a cult.

"What should we tell the other children?" I asked.

"We'll just have to tell them the truth. They'll be upset about it, but it's better for them to know what's going on. They'll know that something is wrong, and that we're worried. It's better if they know why."

"How can we tell Cyndi's friends, or our friends and our families? Who can understand such a thing?" I started to cry again.

Glen stood up and took my hands, pulling me to my feet. "I have some errands to run today, and I want you to come with me. I don't want to leave you here. You can wait in the car while I make a few stops."

I felt too exhausted to argue with him. I didn't want to drive around the city with him while he ran business errands, but I knew that determined tone in his voice. So I put on my coat and went with him.

I sat there in stunned silence while Glen drove. He too, was absorbed in his own thoughts. Glen finished his rounds and we arrived home about the same time the children came home from school. Glen told them about Cyndi rejoining the Children of God. The younger ones were full of questions. "Would she come back to visit? Would she be here for Thanksgiving? What about Christmas?" Eric asked, "Will we ever see her again?"

"The Children of God teach some things that are not true," Glen said. "When she hears these things, she'll know that the Bible doesn't teach that, and she'll come home." The four younger children seemed to accept that explanation. It was Lisa I was worried about. She was disgusted and angry.

"How could Cyndi be so dumb?" she asked. "I'm so sick of her keeping this family in turmoil. When is she going to get herself straightened out so the rest of us can live peaceful lives? I'm so mad at her for this." She looked at Glen and me, tears filling her eyes. "How can she do this to you two? You've been so good to her, you've put up with so much! I'm sorry. I just don't understand her."

With that, she ran to her room and closed the door. I heard her crying, and knocked on her door. "I just want to be by myself for a while," she called out.

Lisa, who was so straight, so self-disciplined, could not understand her older sister.

The next few days were like a nightmare for us. I cried day and night. I would wake in the morning having had only a few

66

hours of fitful sleep. I was unable to take care of my family or myself. Glen was a tower of strength during this time. Although his job demanded his attention, he helped me with the children, insisted that I go with him when he ran errands, and stayed with me as much as possible. But I still cried so much that my eyelids were swollen and chapped.

About the third day, Eric came in from school and found me crying in my room. He sat on the bed next to me and said, "Mommy, are you going to cry all your life?" He looked so worried.

Just then Amy came into the room. "Are you still crying, mom?" she asked. She looked worried too. She kissed me, and sat on the bed next to me. She patted my face and said, "You look so bad mommy, your eyes are so red. Are you ever going to be like you were before? No one is happy here any more. I wish Cyndi would come home so you could stop crying."

Julie and Wendy came in and joined us on the bed.

Julie looked at me and asked, "Mom, don't you love the rest of us?"

"Of course I do!" I answered. "I love all of you very much."

"You seem to be worried only about Cyndi. She's gone, and the rest of us are here. You never talk to us or anything any more. You only cry. It seems that you only love Cyndi."

I realized what I was doing to the rest of my family. Looking at the situation from their point of view, I couldn't blame them for feeling left out.

We sat there and talked for a while, and I told them I was sorry I had been neglecting them these past few days, and that I was going to be better now. I kissed them, and we all went downstairs and started supper.

I did make an effort to keep things going at home, but I was far from over my depression. I just tried to hide it from the children. No more crying in front of them.

My depression turned to self-pity. I began to think back over the past few years, and I went over in my mind all the hard things that had happened in our family. We'd had one thing after another.

I began making a mental list of all the bad things that had happened in my life. I looked back to my childhood, and added to the list from there. All the children's illnesses, the fire that destroyed our home several years earlier, my surgery, Eric's long hospitalization and skin grafts, even the economic recession. It all went on my list. It was an impressive list by any standards, and I rebelled against my circumstances.

I was a born-again believer in Jesus Christ, yet I was questioning God's love for me. I felt that I'd had it! I couldn't take any more. This situation with Cyndi was the last straw. I had "trained her up in the way she should go," as the Bible had told me to. Sure, I made mistakes and wasn't perfect, but I had tried. Now here she was departing from it. The Bible had told me that she would not depart from it. I sank deeper into depression as I went over my list. If this is being a "King's Kid," forget it, I told God. I was not going to speak to Him and I wasn't going to read the Bible any more.

Glen and I had been co-teaching the college age Sunday school class at church, and I felt that under the circumstances, I would have to drop out. One could hardly teach the Bible without reading it. I wouldn't be a hypocrite.

That evening, I told Glen I would not be teaching with him any more, and that I was no longer speaking to God. "Don't expect me to have Bible reading with you," I said, "and don't ask me to pray with you."

I had expected Glen to tell me to shape up, or at least act surprised at such an unusual statement from me, but he just looked at me for a minute and said gently, "I'll do the praying for both of us for a while. God loves you, and He knows how hurt you are right now. In a few days you'll feel better."

I was amazed. How could Glen understand and accept my attitude when I didn't understand it myself? I was horrified that I was having these feelings.

For several days I did not pray, except to remind the Lord that I was not speaking to Him. I was mad at the Lord, and I was mad at Glen and Dr. McLuhan. If they had not told me to let Cyndi go she might still be here.

My anger lashed out in all directions. I blamed myself most of all. I recalled every mistake I had ever made in raising Cyndi. If only I had done this, if only I hadn't done that.

It was a time of self-examination for me. I had tried to raise the children to think for themselves, to be broad-minded, to listen to the other person's point of view. We had taught them that the Lord had given us the Bible as a guideline, we were to use it as a yardstick in everything we did. We were uncompromising on that point. The Lord had not given us the "ten suggestions"; they were commandments. We encouraged the children to examine other people's beliefs, and see how they lined up with the Scriptures. We all had friends of different backgrounds and religions. I had seen so many people raise their children in a cocoon-like atmosphere, where they were never exposed to people who were different. They all talked alike, dressed alike, thought alike. I didn't want that for myself, or for my children.

When I taught eleventh grade girls in the Baptist church, I took them, with their parents' permission, to visit other churches, and to the synagogue. We had a time of dialogue with the rabbi after the service that was very meaningful to the girls, and to me. The study of Judaism was an important prelude to our study of the Apostle Paul and his writings. I enjoyed learning with my class. Glen laughed at me, and called me his "flower child," but he agreed that the children should be exposed to many philosophies, and different kinds of people.

Now here I was with a daughter who had been open-minded, who had listened to the other person's point of view, and she had gotten into a situation where she had been brainwashed , had turned against her family, her school, her church, and been left a very confused and unhappy girl.

I blamed myself for encouraging her open, inquiring mind. She had done what she had been raised to do and it had

69

resulted in this whole mess. If I was so wrong about this, maybe I was wrong about other aspects of child rearing too. I found myself with a lot of doubts about my ability as a parent.

Glen and I had taken the "Institute in Basic Youth Conflicts" seminar at least three or four times. I had read *The Total Woman* and *How to Live Like a King's Kid*, and all the other good books I could find to help me be a better parent with a positive approach to life, a sizzling marriage, and a close walk with the Lord. I was so mad now I wanted to take Bill Gothard's big red notebook, and all my other books, and pitch them in the fireplace. "It doesn't work! None of it works," I told Glen.

I continued in my snit for several more days. Then my ranting and raving settled down. I just went about my work determined to stay away from anything that smacked of religion.

I should have known better than to think the Lord would let go of me that easily. The Holy Spirit followed me around, comforting me. The same sweet Spirit that had drawn me to the Lord so many years earlier was still there. I tried to ignore Him. I kept busy. I played the radio. I went shopping. No matter what I did, or where I went, He was with me. His love almost physically covered me. I had known the *power* of the Holy Spirit in my life, I had known Him as Teacher, and Convictor of sin, but now I knew Him powerfully as the Comforter. That same peace flowed over me, just as it had in our room the night when we first heard Cyndi was missing.

I finally got my eyes off myself, and how I was feeling, and I thought about Glen. He was hurting too. I wanted to be able to comfort him, to reassure him, tell him he had made the right decision in letting her go.

I asked my heavenly Father to forgive me for my rebellious spirit and restore me to a right relationship with Him. He answered my prayer.

I then decided I would try to get a letter to Cyndi, to let her know that we loved her, and that if she should decide to come home, she would always be welcome.

I knew she had a paycheck coming and she would probably go to the store to pick it up the next day. I called the store's personnel department and talked to a lady I knew in the office. I told her what had happened to Cyndi since she had lost her job, and explained that I would like to put a letter in her pay envelope. She was very understanding, and agreed to help me get a letter to Cyndi.

I knew from the attorney general's report that it would be impossible for me to reach Cyndi even if I did know the location of the colony. All the incoming and outgoing mail is read by the shepherd, and it is reported that most of the personal mail is never given to the "babes" in the colony. Especially letters from non-supportive parents.

I was counting on the fact that the colony is interested in a new convert's money almost as much as it is interested in the converts themselves. They probably knew that Cyndi not only had a paycheck due to be paid the next day, but she had a savings account in the credit union as well. I was counting on that money to have kept her in Atlanta. We were told that new converts are never left in their home town for very long, and I felt that once they had her money, they would send her to another state. I had to try to reach her.

That evening I got a call from Rhys Thompson. He was calling from Athens, where he was attending the University of Georgia. He had heard about Cyndi going back with the Children of God, and he wanted us to know her friends up there were praying for her. I thanked him, thinking he'd just called to tell me that he and the others were praying, but he went on to say that he and Todd would be coming to Atlanta to talk with Cyndi.

"We don't know where she is, Rhys. She may not even be in town any more. I'm going to the department store tomorrow to put a letter in with her check and I'm praying she will come in to get it. We want her to know we love her, and she can always come home. I don't want you and Todd to miss classes and come all the way to Atlanta for nothing."

71

"Well, if you don't mind, I'd like to come by and see you in the morning. I feel the Lord is really leading in this matter."

"I'd love to see you, Rhys. If you feel that the Lord has spoken to you, I know you want to be obedient to Him."

The next morning Rhys was at our home just as the younger children were leaving for school. With him were Todd Donetelli, and Shan Gastineau. I knew the Lord was about to do something important in our lives. We all had a feeling of expectancy.

Chapter 10

Glen had an important meeting in the morning and had to go to the office, but he asked me to call him and let him know what was happening. The boys and I visited for a few minutes, then we went to the Lord in prayer.

The phone rang just as we finished praying. It was the lady in the personnel department. She was calling to tell me that Cyndi had called the store a few minutes earlier and told her she would be by later to pick up her check, and close out her savings account. I thanked her and returned to the living room with this good news. They all said, "Praise the Lord!"

On the way to the store, I told the boys a little about the Children of God and their beliefs. The boys had trouble understanding how Cyndi could be talked into such a group. I explained to them what I had been told about the brainwashing that new converts are put through.

The words still sounded strange coming from me. Brainwashing! That word was as foreign to my vocabulary and realm of knowledge as any I could think of. I also explained to them that Cyndi would probably be accompanied by elders from the colony, and that they would try to prevent her from speaking with us. We decided that we would not stay together in the store in case we were seen. We did not intend to kidnap her or try to force her to come with us.

We arrived at the store and I went to the personnel office and gave the letter I had written to the girl at the desk. Everyone at the store was very helpful and understanding. I felt supported from all sides.

After we had waited about an hour, the girl from personnel came to me, and told me that Cyndi was in the office, and had read my letter, and had asked to see me. When I entered the office, Cyndi was sitting there, reading my letter, and crying. When she saw me, she got up and came to me and put her arms around me.

"I love you, mom," she said.

"I love you too, Cyndi. I just had to let you know how much I love you. That's why I had to get that letter to you."

We were crying, and hugging each other. It seemed like an eternity since I had seen her, but it had only been a week.

I got out the Kleenex for both of us, and we were laughing, and crying, and blowing our noses. I looked at Cyndi and saw that she was different. She did not have that hard, belligerent look about her that she had after her first encounter with the Children of God. She looked sweeter, calmer, and seemed more open and less troubled than she had for many months. Her hair was shining and clean. She had a fresh, scrubbed look, and a big smile. She seemed more like her old self now than she had in many months. Oh, how glad I was to see her. How I loved this child of mine. I was so grateful to have a chance to tell her so.

I told Cyndi that Todd, Rhys, and Shan were at the store too. She was pleased and surprised.

"What are they doing in town in the middle of the week?" she asked. I told her about their call to me the night before, and she seemed moved. "I want to see them," she said.

We left the office. Waiting outside the door was a man that I had not noticed on my way in. Cyndi introduced me to him. His name was Ephraim, and he was a "brother," she said. Well, this "brother" was older than I was. He was tall and thin, and had a thick crop of long sandy hair that was greying. His face was lined, and he looked like an old hippie. He seemed disturbed about meeting me, but I was friendly to him, and told him I was glad to meet him. Meanwhile, Cyndi had seen Todd, and when I turned from shaking hands with Ephraim, she and Todd were greeting each other with a hug.

While we were in the inner office, John Hicks, another friend, had come into the store to make a purchase, and had seen Shan and Rhys. They had filled him in on the situation, and he decided to wait and see Cyndi too. Pat Kieper, one of Cyndi's closest friends in high school was there too. Pat worked at the store, and was about to begin her midday shift. I could not have gotten this group together on my own if I had tried. The Lord had really brought about this reunion.

Cyndi was obviously delighted to see these good friends. They had been together last at Bo's birthday party at our home during the summer. This group of friends were close and got together as much as possible. Since graduation, however, they had gone off to different schools, and their meetings were becoming few and far between.

I asked all of them if they would like to come to the house for lunch and visit for a while. I was careful to indicate that Ephraim was invited too. Ephraim said no, they could not come with us, they did not have permission from the shepherd.

Cyndi said, "Oh, we can call him from my house." Without waiting for a reply, she started walking toward the door, talking a mile a minute to her friends, leaving Ephraim to follow along. He looked a bit frustrated.

I had called Glen from the store, telling him that Cyndi was there, and would be coming home for lunch. Now he was in the parking lot and he drove about half of this happy group back to our house. Rhys drove the rest of the group, and we all met back at our house. Glen picked up some Kentucky Fried Chicken, and we all prepared to have lunch.

Glen and Cyndi were especially happy to see each other. The look of relief and joy on Glen's face said he was glad to have his daughter back. He took Cyndi by the hand. They stepped out of the room for just a minute to have a private word with each other. This seemed to upset Ephraim, who got up from the couch and looked down the hall after them.

During lunch the conversation was light, and no one mentioned the Children of God.

John had recently had surgery for a bleeding ulcer, and was not in school this quarter. We all inquired about his health. The other boys teased him, telling him that some people would do anything to get out of going to school. There was a lighthearted, almost festive mood.

The phone rang, and it was for Cyndi. It was the shepherd, calling to tell her to return at once to the colony. We could hear her telling him that she had not seen these friends in a long time, and she would like to visit with them for a while longer.

Cyndi returned to the table and resumed her conversation with her friends. A few minutes later the phone rang again, and it was the shepherd calling again, this time to speak to Ephraim. They spoke for about five minutes, then Ephraim called Cyndi to the phone again. We could hear her talking, and she sounded annoyed. We heard her say, "These are my Christian brothers, too. The family is not the only Christian group, you know." She was arguing with the shepherd.

Cyndi returned to the table once more, but did not tell us what her conversation on the phone had been about.

Shan had been quiet during lunch, and I could feel his disapproval of the whole situation. He was an intense young man, not one for small talk, and I could sense that he wanted to get to the business at hand, and discuss the cult.

I turned to Ephraim and said, "Tell me about the Children of God, Ephraim. I've heard and read some pretty negative things about the group, and I would be interested in hearing what you think about the ministry."

"He seemed glad to have a chance to talk. He put down his napkin, and sat back in his chair. "What would you like to know?" he asked.

"Well, tell me what brought you to the group, for instance, and what the appeal was for you. How does it meet your needs, spiritually and so forth."

He then embarked on a discourse about the errors of the organized church, higher education, politics, society in general, and especially family life. He told us that to have a family such as ours was showing favoritism to the people who are related to us. Such favoritism, he said, was sinful.

The phone rang again, and Cyndi said, "If that's for me, I don't want to talk right now."

Glen got up from the table, and said, "I'll take the call." It was the shepherd again, and he asked to speak to Cyndi. Glen said, "This is her father, may I help you?"

The shepherd said, "No, I need to speak to Cyndi. It's very important."

"What's the problem?" Glen asked.

"The problem is that Cyndi and Ephraim are to return to the colony at once. You cannot hold them there against their will."

"No one is holding anyone against their will," Glen said. "We're just finishing lunch, and when they're ready to leave, someone will drive them back to the colony."

The shepherd said, "Let me speak to Cyndi."

"She does not wish to speak to you right now," Glen said. "Let me take your number, and I'll ask her to return your call in a few minutes."

"No, I won't give you the number. Ephraim has it, she can get it from him. Tell them to call me back right away."

Glen returned to the table, and gave Ephraim and Cyndi the message.

While Glen had been on the phone with the shepherd, Ephraim had been telling me about the error of our life style.

"This kind of family setup is of the devil," he went on. "God never intended for us to live like this. Jesus even told his own family to get lost."

"Really?" I said. "Where is that found in the Bible?"

"Do you people have a Bible around here?" he asked.

Cyndi smiled at that question. We all had a couple of Bibles, and we joked about being "Bible poor." Someone was always coming home with a new translation.

I said, "Yes, we have a Bible."

"Do you have a King James Version?" he asked.

I said we did, and went and got him the Bible from the other room.

All eyes were on Ephraim as he paged through the Bible looking for this passage that would prove to us that Jesus did not approve of traditional family life styles, and had in fact, told his own parents to "get lost." He turned to Luke 2:49, and before he started to read, he asked all of us if we remembered the story of Jesus in the temple, and how Mary and Joseph had to return to Jerusalem to look for him. We all nodded. He began reading, "And he said unto them, How is it that ye sought me? wist ye not that I must be about my Father's business?" Ephraim looked at us and said, "You see, Jesus put his Father's work above the demands that his family put on him, and he set them straight when he was only a child of twelve."

I looked at him and said, "Read on, Ephraim."

"What do you mean?"

"Read the rest of the passage."

Ephraim looked very confused. His hand was shaking as he held the Bible.

Glen said, "If you'll read the rest of that passage, you'll see that you were reading it out of context. Go on and see what He did then."

Ephraim, looking very shaken read on. "And they understood not the saying which he spoke unto them. And he went down with them, and came to Nazareth, and was subject unto them: but his mother kept all these sayings in her heart. And Jesus increased in wisdom and stature, and in favor with God and man." Ephraim read it again to himself, as if he had never seen that portion of Scripture before. He had been given Scripture out of context, and had made false assumptions about what it meant.

With that, Cyndi looked at Ephraim and said, "That's what you people have been doing all week! You take Scripture out of context, and twist the word of God to meet your own needs! I'm not going back there. I belong here with my family. I've been such a fool, but this week has really cured me of Children of God once and for all. Would someone drive me to the colony to get my clothes, and take Ephraim back?"

Glen said he'd be glad to drive her, and the boys said that they would be glad to also. Ephraim said that Cyndi should go on with her friends, and he asked Glen if he would mind taking him. He explained that he needed to stop somewhere along the way. Glen said that he'd be glad to take him anywhere he needed to go, and they all got up and left.

Glen told me later, that Ephraim had him stop at a pay phone, and that Ephraim had talked to someone for about fifteen minutes before Glen took him back to the commune.

Cyndi returned home that afternoon and we all rejoiced. The Lord had used Todd, Rhys and Shan to bring Cyndi back. We really had so much to praise the Lord for. He had again answered our prayers, and had done it all in such an unusual way.

The boys had seen the hand of the Lord in this situation as they had been obedient to Him. Their faith was made even stronger through this experience. The happenings of the day had a profound effect on all of us.

When the other children came in from school, they were really happy to see Cyndi. They hugged and kissed each other like they had been separated for a year.

After dinner, we all gathered in the family room and talked. Instead of retreating into her room like she had for the past few months. Cyndi joined us, and seemed like her old self again. She was all smiles, and very talkative.

The other children started asking her questions about the colony. I was a little worried that this would upset Cyndi, as it had in the past, but she was receptive to their questions, and answered them without the least bit of irritation.

"What did you do all day in the colony?" Amy asked.

"We got up, and did our chores, and had Bible studies, and ate, and went out all day selling tracts, and tried to get new converts to the group," she told us.

"Did you like it there?" Eric asked her.

"Not really," she answered. "I missed all of you too much."

"We cried about you being gone," Amy told her. "Did you ever cry about us?"

Cyndi looked at us. "Yes, I cried at night, because I knew I had made a mistake. I didn't belong there."

She looked at Glen and said, "Every morning, the first thought that came into my head was, 'My father hates the Children of God.' "

Glen got up from where he was sitting and sat next to Cyndi on the couch. He put his arm around her and said, "I'm just glad you came home to us."

Julie asked her, "Did they give you a different name again?"

Cyndi said yes, it was a different name this time. She told us that the names were changed sometimes, especially if the family of the new convert knew the name, and if the family did not like their child being in the commune.

The children were full of questions, and Cyndi was answering them all, and didn't seem the least bit perturbed.

Cyndi was describing how all the girls slept in one room, and the boys slept in another room, and the married couples each had a room together. She told them that the life in the colony was very disciplined, and everyone worked very hard.

Lisa was sitting on the fireplace hearth, not saying much, and when Cyndi finished describing life in the colony, Lisa just shook her head. "I can't believe that you could be interested in such a group, Cyndi. It sounds like a bunch of little kids playing commune. Kind of like when we were little and played house or store. It's so dumb, so childish. I can't imagine a bunch of people your age leaving home like that and sitting around a dumpy house in a bad neighborhood saying, 'Now your name will be Sarah, and your name will be Adam, and we'll all live here together and hide from our parents, and talk bad about everyone who isn't in our little group.' "

Lisa's pragmatic evaluation of the communal life style

seemed to embarrass Cyndi somewhat.

"It sure sounds dumb when you put it that way," Cyndi said sheepishly. "I feel pretty silly about the whole thing."

The younger children went to bed, and Glen and Cyndi and I stayed up late talking. With the younger children out of the room, Cyndi opened up further, and told us about her week, and how she had decided even before seeing the boys and me at the store, that she was going to leave the Children of God.

"I've had a terrible week," she said. "I stayed in trouble with the shepherd all week. We were taught from Mo letters, and some of them were so badly misleading, with Scripture taken out of context, that I just had to speak up. The shepherd kept warning me that I should not argue with him, and I should not question the word of Moses, and his divine inspiration.

"This morning I was given a book to read called *Free Sex*. In this book there were many Mo letters, mostly on sex, and I was told to read to a certain place, then stop. Well, you know how fast I read. I finished the first few that I was told to read, and I just flipped through the rest of them, kind of scanning them, and I saw one in the back of the book called *Women in Love*. It was really awful. It said that lesbianism is okay. Mo said in this letter that if two women fall in love, it would be all right for them to marry. It's better to marry a guy, he said, because we need to be having babies to build a nation, but if women are in love, they may marry.

"Well, I threw that book across the room. When the shepherd came in and saw me throwing that book against the wall, he cleared the room, and told everyone else to go to another part of the house. He asked me what had upset me this time, and I told him that I had read *Women in Love*.

" 'You weren't supposed to read that,' he told me. 'You're not ready for that yet.'

"I told him that I *never* would be ready for that kind of perversion, and I got out my Bible, and read to him what the Lord has to say about homosexuals. I told him it's an abomination to the Lord. It says so in the Old Testament, and

81

in the New Testament, and nothing that anybody else says about it can change the word of God.

"He told me that I was not obedient or submissive, and I would be disciplined if I continued to disrupt the Bible studies, and argue with Mo's teachings. He said that we would have to have a talk this evening about my attitude."

I said, "Cyndi, you don't seem to be confused or disoriented this time, like you were last time you went with the group. How do you explain that?"

"I went in of my own free will this time, and they did not put me through the indoctrination that I went through in Chattanooga. I had my guard up, and remembered all I had heard about the group. They really didn't treat me like a babe this time. The colony here in Atlanta is a model colony and it was run according to the rule book. Proper sleep, hard work, cleanliness, no drinking, better food. They use this colony as an example to try to get others to join. They want to make it as appealing as possible."

"What do you mean, no drinking?" Glen asked.

"In the colony in Chattanooga, they drank a lot of beer. In fact, the colony in Chattanooga was really different than the one here. Up there, they would go on a picnic, or go to a movie sometimes instead of going out to 'litness.' Everything was just hanging loose there. They really run a tight ship here. I got to see the real thing in this Atlanta colony."

Cyndi told us that she was scheduled to leave Atlanta for Denver in the next few days. They planned to use her to teach in the Montessori schools set up by the Children of God for the many children born to family members. They did not plan for her to stay in Denver long though, just a brief training period, then she would be sent to Sweden.

"Why Sweden?" we asked.

"Because of my Swedish background, I suppose."

She then told us that the Children of God are moving to Europe as fast as they can. They are being persecuted here in

America, they told her. America is about to fall anyway, and they are taught this daily. They call America an "old whore."

During the next few days, we were to learn many things about life in the colony. Cyndi described the crude skits put on nightly by the senior members. The skits always portrayed the Children of God as superior to the rest of society, and with dramatic dances and costumes, and plays, they depicted money, education, and the organized church as evil.

She told us of a young man coming out in a green and white leotard and green and white make-up, depicting money, doing all manner of evil. Another skit had a young man laden with signs on chains around his neck. The signs said, "car payments, family obligations, school, church activities, rent," and so forth. There was a big box in the middle of the stage, and written on the box was "college." The boy was put into the box by people labeled "parents," and the box was closed. Another boy labeled "system" jumped on the box and shouted, "Now we've got him!"

One of the most dramatic skits was that of a young man dressed as a Russian Cossack dancer. He danced for several minutes whirling and kicking with the aid of loud recorded music, and professional lighting. After a few minutes of this, he stopped and started talking to his audience. He called them comrades, and challenged them to get the same fervor that the comrades of the sixties had. They were better comrades then, he accused. He went on to extoll the virtues of communism, and the evils of democracy and capitalism. Then they all got up and danced to the Russian folk music late into the night.

Within the commune, Cyndi was told not to wear her cross. When she asked why, the shepherd responded, "If Jesus had died in the electric chair would you wear one around your neck?" She was given a yoke on a chain to wear instead. She was told that it was the yoke of the servant of the Lord.

Even the coffee mugs in the commune had the Mo letter cartoon characters and "Mo quotes" on them. It was total saturation with Mo and his teachings.

After hearing about all this, we weren't surprised that people who knew less about Scripture than Cyndi did were deceived by the claims and promises of the Children of God. But we were most of all grateful that Cyndi had come out of the commune of her own free will, and was now home with us.

Chapter 11

The road back to a normal, sane life was not an easy one for Cyndi or the rest of us. She was back home, but a lot of healing had yet to take place. Cyndi's level of maturity was still far below that of a girl of nineteen, and she was in a highly suggestible state of mind, due to the brainwashing that she had been put through. David Brubaker suggested that we allow him to deprogram her, and have her go through a period called rehabilitation. We still resisted the idea of deprogramming, and we felt sure in time Cyndi would be her old self again. David was not able to give us much information about what was involved in deprogramming, and we just didn't want to put Cyndi through any more traumas. We were just glad to have her back home.

Some of Cyndi's friends made it clear they thought she had been pretty gullible to fall for such a group. Except for the first day or two back at home, she seldom referred to her time with the group. She began to feel that she had been pretty dumb. Nothing we could say to her seemed to make her feel any better. She avoided her friends, and slipped back into the same reclusive type of life that she had adopted after her first encounter with the group in Tennessee.

She was depressed and withdrawn. Her attitude at home was just awful. When she did join the family, she would bicker with the younger children, and sass me and her father. We had many quarrels. We had never been a family to take rudeness from our children, and we were not about to start now. We told her so, but it didn't seem to get through. We were at a loss to know what to do about this situation. It was affecting our family life and putting a terrible strain on all of us.

Cyndi still had a rebellious attitude toward church and the government. She refused to attend church with the family, and she told us that she was a socialist. I worried about the effect of all her negative comments on the younger children. It wasn't long before Wendy decided that she didn't like to go to church either, and we had a problem getting everyone up and out on Sunday morning. We explained to Wendy that we all go to church on Sunday, and she would go too. She grudgingly got dressed, declaring that when she was nineteen, like Cyndi, she wouldn't go to church either.

Cyndi decided to go to Georgia State University for the winter quarter. We were glad that she had decided to do something constructive.

One afternoon she came in and was in a better mood than usual. I said, "Hi hon, how was your day?"

"Pretty good. Two of the sororities have asked me to teas and parties. Going to a state school sure is different than a small Christian school. You see everything there."

"I suppose you do. Do you like it?"

"It's okay. I went to a meeting of the young socialist party today."

I just looked at her. I was longing for the days of Campus Crusade meetings, choir practice, and rehearsals for plays. I wasn't sure I was ready for this, and I knew that Glen was less ready than I was. Glen's politics are pretty conservative, and he teasingly called me "bleeding heart" when he felt that I was too liberal. We had always discussed politics, and tried to inform the children about what was going on. We encouraged them to think for themselves, and form opinions of their own. Glen and I seldom agreed on politics, and had been known to cancel each other out at the polls. But Cyndi a socialist? I tried to look casual as I asked her to tell me about it.

"You wouldn't believe those kids, mom. They're wild. They all had Castro-type beards and hats and jackets. They're so militant and full of hate. It scared me to death." She took a sip of her coffee. Looking thoughtful, she said, "Maybe I'm not a socialist."

"Really?" I said. "What are you?"

"I guess I'm a democrat," she said.

We had not wanted to worry Glen's mother by telling her about Cyndi's involvement with the cult, so when she came to Atlanta for a visit, we filled her in on what had happened.

Cyndi had been especially close to her grandparents. We lived in Iron Mountain, Michigan for the first few years of Cyndi's life, having moved there when she was only seven weeks old. Glen's mom had been a big help to me in raising Cyndi. She was much more than a mother-in-law to me. She was, and is, my good friend. She never gave advice unless it was asked for, and even then, she was reluctant to give it. After we moved away, grandma came and stayed with the other children when I had a new baby. She had a way of making me feel her approval. I never could understand mother-in-law jokes. My relationship with Glen's parents was something I treasured.

I had a lot of admiration for Glen's mother for the way she handled the loss of her husband. Glen's father was a dynamic Christian man, full of life and fun. When he died suddenly, it left a void in all of our lives that could never be filled. After a brief but serious depression Glen's mom pulled herself together, sold the house in the country and bought a smaller one in town. She learned to drive a car, and rode in a plane for the first time. She even went to Sweden with her sister to visit relatives there, and to visit her birthplace. This was a lady with a lot of spunk. She had made a new life for herself and everyone admired her courage.

We all tried to make grandma's visit with us as pleasant as possible, but still the tension could be felt.

Grandma looked surprised when Cyndi did not attend church with us, but she didn't comment. The younger children grumbled about Cyndi not having to do the things that they had to do.

One morning Cyndi and I had an argument, and after all the children had left for school, and grandma had gotten up, we had a late breakfast together. We were lingering over our second cup of coffee when she looked at me and said, "Why don't you tell me what's bothering you?"

I had been on the verge of tears all morning, and with that the waterworks really started. After I blew my nose, I told her about the feelings I was having, my doubts about my ability as a mother, and my frustration in not knowing how to handle the situation. "Maybe I've been too permissive," I said.

"You've never been what I would call a permissive mother," she said.

"Well, maybe I've been too strict. I only know that things are not going well in this home, and if I'm not responsible, who is? Right now I feel as if I've lost the war, and don't know where to go to surrender."

"You've been a good mother. You've done a good job of raising these children. They've been brought up in the church, and you've given them so much love. No child could ask for more. You and Glen are good parents, and you should quit blaming yourselves for Cyndi's mistakes.

"When I was a girl and someone went through a period like this, we said that they were going over 'fool's hill.' They have a lot of fancy, high-sounding names for it now, but it's still 'fool's hill.' I went over that hill, and so did you. We all do. It's part of growing up. Some of us take longer than others, but we all get to the other side eventually, and so will Cyndi."

I had never heard of "fool's hill" before, but I knew that I had been over it too. Some of us just aren't so public about it.

"I appreciate that," I told her. "It means a lot to me, knowing you think I've been a good mother. How many women hear that from their mother-in-law?"

"You're probably right too about it just being a phase that Cyndi's going through. But until she gets over it, how do I deal with the day-to-day tension, and the effect on the other children?"

"You know, Lee, when a baby bird gets too big for the nest, the mother bird pushes it out, and it has to learn to fly on its own."

I couldn't believe what I was hearing. Cyndi is one of grandma's favorite people in the world, and here she was telling me to kick her out!

"But she can't support herself yet," I protested. "She isn't trained to do anything except part-time work. She couldn't afford an apartment, and a car, and all the other expenses that it would take to start out on her own."

"If Cyndi can't make it on her own, then she should fit in with the plans of the rest of the family," Glen's mother said. "Either she's a member of the family, doing what everyone else is doing, or she should give up her plan for a college education and room with a girl friend. She can do a lot of things without a college education. I think it's time you put your foot down. You're very nervous, and the other children are being affected."

I couldn't believe what I was hearing. This sweet lady who always went out of her way to stay out of her grown children's business, was really counseling me. She poured another cup of coffee and we continued our conversation.

"You know," she went on, "when Cyndi was growing up, you were free of this kind of tension. You didn't have distractions to keep you upset and worried. Don't you think the other children deserve a calm mother, too? Cyndi is grown. Now you must concentrate on the other children. I don't mean turn your back on Cyndi. Just consider her an adult who should take responsibility for her own actions, and live with the consequences."

I thought over what grandma had said as I cleaned up the kitchen. She was right. Our home was disrupted. I was nervous. The younger children did need my attention. But I couldn't let Cyndi go off on her own when I knew she was not emotionally or financially ready for such a move. I knew we had a problem, but I still didn't have the answer.

When Cyndi came in from school that afternoon, I heard her and grandma talking in the living room about Cyndi possibly getting an apartment with a girl friend. They talked for quite a while, and I could hear what they were saying as I prepared supper. It was much the same conversation grandma and I had had earlier in the day. I wondered if Cyndi was as surprised as I had been in getting such direct counseling from her grandmother.

A few days later, grandma went back home. When we took her to the airport, she kissed us good-bye, and told us that she would be praying for all of us.

"Remember," she said, "the Scripture that says 'Train up a child in the way he should go and when he is old he will not depart from it.' Cyndi is not old yet."

After the visit with her grandmother, Cyndi began to change. One day I said, "Cyndi, you really are getting back to your old sweet self."

"I guess my talk with grandma really helped me to see how messed up I was. If grandma thought I needed shaping up, I must really need shaping up. I'm trying to do better."

Cyndi's guitar had been in its case, untouched for many months. As I was coming up the steps one day, I heard her softly strumming it. No singing, as she used to, just strumming. I felt such joy well up in me, and I just praised the Lord for continuing to heal her and restore her to her former self.

The next Sunday Cyndi came downstairs dressed for church. "Are you going to church with us?" I asked.

"No, I'm going to start looking around for a church near home. I promised grandma that I would go to church somewhere. I can't be a bad influence on the younger kids." She looked at her dad and me. "Do you have any suggestions?"

We both named a couple of churches nearby and she went

out visiting. We were delighted to see her trying so hard and we were pleased that she had asked our opinion.

Cyndi shared with us later that when she read the Bible she would have thoughts about the Children of God, and she would get upset. She had the same problem in church. Some portion of Scripture, or a song would make her feel as she had when she was in the Children of God, and it was very upsetting to her. We did not know till later, that this is a typical problem for kids coming out of the cults. It takes about a year for them to overcome this.

Cyndi came home from church one Sunday all smiles. "I've found my church!" she announced.

"It's Providence Presbyterian, the one you like so much, mom. It's so neat! I just love the pastor and his wife. What a sermon I heard this morning! It was just what I needed. Pastor Mulford preached that sermon just for me."

"What was it about?" we asked.

"Well, I could never say it like Rev. Mulford, but he talked about how nothing could ever happen to us that had not been filtered through God's love. Everything that comes into our lives has to be approved by the Lord. He can turn even the worst situations around and use them for His honor and glory. Even this mess about the Children of God could probably be used somehow. I can't see how, but I'm just asking God to use even this."

Cyndi had been attending Providence for about a month when she was asked by Kathy, the pastor's wife, if she would be interested in working with the youth in the church. They had a need for someone to teach the junior high Sunday school class, and to help with the socials.

This was right up Cyndi's alley, and she agreed to take on the job. She joined the church, and began to work with the youth, throwing herself into the work wholeheartedly. In a few weeks, she had started a choir, and had a bimonthly newsletter going out to all the young people. Cyndi was getting her life back in order. Instead of spending all her time in her room, she was

91

now organizing socials, preparing lessons, making posters, and enjoying every minute of it.

People began to ask her to speak in churches about the cult, to sound a warning to others about the dangers of talking to these street evangelists, and going to Bible studies, or parties with them. Cyndi accepted the invitations to speak, but would come home really worn out. It seemed to be a mushrooming thing. Word had gotten around, and Cyndi was asked more and more to speak to groups of young people. She was even interviewed on a national radio program sponsored by the Church of Christ, and was a guest on a local radio talk show.

Every time she spoke, she would come home and say, "Never again. I just get too exhausted and I hate reliving the experience."

"Don't do it then," I said. "You don't have to accept any more invitations to speak. Do only what you're comfortable with. I know that people are interested in what happened to you, and they appreciate the firsthand information that you have about the cults, but you've done quite a bit to enlighten people already. Maybe this would be a good time to forget your experience, and turn down further invitations to speak. I get weary of the subject myself, and I just want life to go on in a normal way again."

"That's what I want, too," she said, "but someone has to warn people about the dangers of the cults. If someone had told me about them, I wouldn't have gone with them, or even talked to them when they stopped me on the street. I'm really torn. On the one hand, I want to just forget the Children of God, yet I feel a real need to warn people. I keep asking myself, what does the Lord want me to do? If I can just keep one person from joining, it will be worth it. I just wish there was someone else to do it."

I could understand her conflict. She was getting herself back to normal more and more, and she wanted to be just your average, carefree, nineteen-year-old. Yet she knew that she had a unique message that could possibly save another from a tragic mistake.

"I know you'll make the right decision," I told her.

"I know the Lord wants me to tell about my experience, but I just hate to get up in front of a group of people and admit that I was so dumb." With that she crossed her eyes, and made a face, and mocked herself. "I'm the dummy who went off with a bunch of weirdos and got my head messed up."

We both laughed at her antics. Cyndi's sense of humor was returning.

Chapter 12

It was my birthday, and I was feeling good as I prepared dinner for my family. I smiled to myself as I got a glimpse of Amy and Eric sneaking down the steps and into the downstairs bedroom. They had something covered with a towel. A birthday present for me, no doubt. They had wrapping paper, scissors, and ribbon. Julie motioned them into her room, and they closed the door. Julie was known as the number one wrapper at our house, and the younger children could count on her to help with gift wrapping. The children got so much pleasure out of giving gifts. Almost as much as receiving them, I thought. Almost.

Things were really getting back to normal around our house. Cyndi still had some problems she was working through, but life was not the roller coaster existence that it had been for so long. I was so grateful to the Lord for bringing us through such a hard place and getting us back on solid ground.

Lisa came in to help me with dinner. "Oh, I forgot to tell you mom. While you were out, a lady called you. I have her number here. She wants you to call her back as soon as possible. It's something about the Children of God. She said her daughter joined them, and she wants to know more about the group." She handed me the number.

"I better call her right back. I wonder how she got our name," I said, half to myself. Lisa told me that our church had given it to her.

I noticed the number Lisa handed me had the same exchange as ours. "These people must live around here," I said as I dialed the number.

Charlotte Joh was a soft-spoken woman, but I could hear the concern in her voice as she told me that her twenty-two-year-old daughter had joined the Children of God.

"I understand you've had a similar experience, and you have some information about the group. A report from the attorney general?"

"Yes, we do have some information, and we'd be glad to share it with you. Could you come by and get it?"

"We'd appreciate that so much," Charlotte said. "Should we come now? I notice that our phone exchange is the same. We must live in the same part of town."

I told her where we lived, and we were both amazed. We lived just a few blocks from each other. She told me where her house was, and I realized that we had walked by their house many times and had admired the beautiful landscaping and vegetable garden.

Glen came in just as I finished giving Charlotte directions to our house. I got a big kiss, and a hug from Glen, and he sang happy birthday to me, the children joining in.

"Thank you, thank you," I said, bowing elaborately. "You all sure are enthused about me getting older." I got hugs and kisses from all of them.

"I just got a call from a lady who lives near here whose daughter has joined the Children of God. I hope you don't mind waiting awhile for dinner. I invited them to come over to pick up the attorney general's report. I think they need to talk to someone."

Everyone agreed that we should hold dinner, and talk to the Johs.

Glen talked to me in the kitchen, leaning on the counter, while I put the finishing touches on supper.

"Hon, remember how I felt when people tried to tell us about the Children of God? I thought they were crazy."

Glen smiled as he munched on an apple.

I went on, "I thought we had run into a bunch of loonies. How much do you think we should tell them?"

"We have to give them the whole story," Glen said. "The attorney general's report will be the biggest help. Remember, we didn't have that report till so much later. We had already been through the worst of it by the time we got that."

Glen was right, the report would add credibility to what we would be telling them.

A short time later, the doorbell rang, and we welcomed a handsome, well-dressed couple. With them were their son, Fritz, and Charlotte's brother, Buddy Creel. Charlotte was a pretty blonde with a dazzling smile and Lee was a distinguished looking man with greying sideburns, and a moustache.

It was Buddy who had called our church and talked to Dr. McLuhan. Buddy was a minister, and he knew the staff there. Dr. Mac told Buddy that we had been through a similar experience, and we could probably give them more information than he could. He told Buddy that the Children of God were false prophets, and a "diabolical group."

We visited with the Johs for a few minutes, and found we had much more in common with them than a daughter involved in a cult. They, like us, had majored in girls. Fritz was the only boy in a family of five children, while we had one boy in a family of six children.

Fritz was twenty-four years old, and a recent graduate of Georgia Tech. He was a handsome young man with sandy colored hair, and a neatly trimmed beard and moustache. Glen and Fritz, both being engineers, chatted a few minutes about their jobs, then we got to the subject of the Children of God.

The Johs told us about Pennee, their youngest child and what had taken place over the past few days. Pennee, they said, was an airline stewardess, twenty-two years old, and had been on her own since she was eighteen. They described an outgoing, bright girl who had lots of friends, who had always been stable and close to her family.

The Johs told us they were Lutheran and that the children had been raised in the church and had been active Christians all their lives.

Pennee was between roommates, and had moved in with her brother, Fritz. Since they both traveled, neither he nor Pennee were home very much. Fritz told us Pennee had seemed upset lately. Her boyfriend was talking about getting married, but he was not a believer, and this bothered her. Fritz told us that he and Pennee were both at home a few weekends ago. She was reading *The Late Great Planet Earth*, and was growing concerned about her Christian life. Pennee wanted to know more about the Bible, and the second coming of Christ. Fritz told us he was feeling badly now that he had not spent more time with her.

This was obviously a close-knit, loving Christian family. We understood how they were feeling. We had been there. They had no idea where their daughter was now, only that she had joined some far-out cult.

They told us they had gotten a call at two-thirty in the morning from one of Pennee's friends, telling them that Pennee had quit her job, and was joining a group of people who lived in a commune. The friend said that Pennee was acting very strangely, and she felt she should call them even though it was so late. Charlotte than called Pennee and asked her what was going on. Pennee talked to her mother on the phone, and sounded quite normal, except she didn't know what day it was. Pennee seemed to have forgotten that both of her parents worked, and suggested meeting them in the morning. When she was reminded by her mother that it was Monday morning, and they would be at work, Pennee seemed surprised it was Monday already.

While Pennee was talking to her mother on the phone, Fritz came in. He had found a note pinned to the aquarium in the front hall. The note told him that Pennee would be leaving with a group called the Children of God. It was signed Rebecca.

Fritz took the phone, and told his mother there was a young man and a woman sleeping in sleeping bags in the living room. Since Fritz was there, the Johs decided to wait until morning to go and talk to Pennee.

After a restless night Charlotte called her brother, Buddy, and they made plans to go to see Pennee later on in the morning. They prayed together on the phone, asking God to protect Pennee and keep her in His care.

Lee, Buddy and Charlotte arrived at Pennee's home about eight in the morning. They found the door unlocked, and just walked in. Fritz had gone to work. They looked around, and, not seeing anyone, went upstairs. There in Pennee's room, they found Pennee and a girl named "Mary Magdalene," sitting in the middle of Pennee's bed with an open Bible. They were having some sort of Bible lesson. A young man who was introduced as "Pilgrim" had been shaving in Fritz's bathroom. After the introductions, Charlotte suggested they all go downstairs and have some breakfast. Pennee pointed to the open Bible and said, "This is my food."

"Let's go downstairs, anyway," Lee said. "We want to talk to you."

Downstairs, Pennee told her parents that she was giving her life to Christ, and she would be serving Him full-time. Lee and Charlotte tried to question Pennee about her decision, but Pennee would look at Pilgrim for the answers. He did the talking for her. Charlotte challenged this by asking Pennee why she couldn't answer for herself. Again, she looked to Pilgrim. The Johs could see that Pennee was under his complete control. They were also concerned about the strange look in Pennee's eyes, and the odd, slow way she moved.

The Johs suggested to Pennee that she come home with them for the day. Charlotte said, "Let's go home and build a fire and sit down and talk things over." Pilgrim quickly told them it would be impossible for Pennee to do that. An argument started, and the Johs called the police. It was apparent to them that Pennee was not in control of her own mind, and they didn't know what to do.

The police arrived, and after hearing the story, told the Johs that since Pennee was twenty-two years old, she would have to make up her own mind about what to do with her life. Pilgrim told the Johs and Buddy to leave. The police asked whose home it was, and the Johs told them that their son, Fritz, owned the condominium. The phone rang just then, and it was Fritz.

The police talked to him on the phone and asked him who should leave. He said that Pilgrim and Mary Magdalene should leave.

The police told them they had to leave. When they went out the door Lee went with them and tried to take Pennee by force into his car. The police stopped him, telling him that he couldn't do that. Pennee was of age, and she could go with these people if she wanted to. Pennee drove off with Pilgrim and Mary Magdalene.

Charlotte, her face showing the stress of the day, said, "If Pennee had told us she was going to become a missionary, and if she were doing so through a recognized church, we would be thrilled. We would do all we could to support her in that decision. But this anti-parent doctrine that they spout is not scriptural. It's not right, not any of it."

The Johs told us they had been on the phone most of the day trying to get information about the Children of God, but until they reached Dr. McLuhan, they had not been successful. They felt the Lord had led them to us. We felt that way too.

We had been listening to their story with much interest. We had been through such a similar experience. It was all so bizarre. Where does one turn for help at a time like this?

"What can you tell us about this group?" Lee Joh asked.

"We have a report, as we mentioned before. We'd be glad to give it to you," Glen said. "We can also tell you what happened to us, and how we worked through it, if that will help."

I said, "You know, when people started telling me about the group, I thought they were crazy. Stories of brainwashing, mind control and hypnotism just did not seem like twentieth-century America. It's true, though. They capture the minds of these young people, and they very quickly have them under their complete domination."

Charlotte sat forward on the sofa, wringing her hands. "If I had not seen Pennee this morning, I wouldn't have believed that she could be so changed in such a short space of time, but the girl that we saw at the condominium was not anything like the former Pennee. She was like a stranger to us—completely dominated by that Pilgrim person. It had to be hypnotism or something. How could they do that so quickly?"

"I don't know how they do it," I said, "just that it is done, and very quickly."

We then gave them a brief account of what happened to Cyndi.

"What should we do?" Lee asked. "We can't just let Pennee stay with those people. Where do you think they took her?"

Then Cyndi came home from work. We introduced her to the Johs, and filled her in on what happened to Pennee, and how they had come to know of us.

Cyndi was very concerned. She talked to the Johs, answering questions, and asking some about Pennee.

"They probably took her to the model colony on Virginia Avenue," Cyndi told them. "That's where I was the second time I joined the group. They take most of the babes there for indoctrination. You'll never get her to come out on her own. You'll have to grab her when she's out witnessing." Cyndi got right to the heart of the problem and came up with a solution as only an impetuous nineteen-year-old could.

Fritz jumped right on that idea. He and Cyndi talked about the location of the colony, the habits of the "family," and their comings and goings. He wrote down the address that Cyndi gave him, and he decided he would go to the commune that night. He said he'd pretend to be interested in joining himself, and gain entrance that way.

Cyndi looked at him. "You look awfully straight to try that," she teased. "Just don't tell them you're an engineer. They'd

101

never buy it. We were taught that engineers and hard hats are the worst kind of systemites."

Fritz found this amusing. "I'm a hard hat, too," he grinned. "I'm working on turbines in my job, and I have to wear a hard hat when inspecting jobs."

Cyndi groaned. "The Lord will really have to take charge on this one. Your beard will help some." Cyndi had brought a moment of lightness to this tense situation, and we all chuckled.

I was worried about Fritz trying to trick these slick operators. Charlotte was concerned, too. None of us wanted Fritz to get involved. He was certainly a very bright young man with both feet on the ground, but he would be dealing with people who were highly trained and skilled at a job of recruiting and controlling young people.

"What do you think we ought to do?" Charlotte asked.

We all sat there for a moment, then I said, "I think we ought to pray about it, and ask the Lord to give us wisdom."

We bowed our heads, and Buddy led us in prayer. Several of us prayed and asked the Lord to guide us. Charlotte prayed and rededicated her life to Christ there in our living room. None of us knew how this would turn out, but we were all sure that we had the source of all wisdom and power in God, and that He would answer our prayers.

Chapter 13

They got up to leave, and as we walked them to the door, Charlotte turned to me and gave me a hug. "I just thank God that He led us to you," she said. "We just didn't know where to turn. Thank you for seeing us and talking with us."

"We're glad we could be here to talk to you," I said. "There were people here and in Chattanooga who dropped everything to help us, and it's nice to be able to pass it on. I don't know how much help we can give you, but we'll do anything we can to help you get your daughter back. If she's been seeking the Lord, as you've said, He surely wouldn't want her to stay with the Children of God. He'll show you how to get her out."

Fritz told us he would go to the commune right away. "Is it okay if I come back later this evening and talk to you some more? I'd like to tell you what I've found out."

"Please do. We'll be up late, so come back and let us know," Glen said. "Be careful."

With that, the Johs left, and we had a late birthday dinner.

About eleven o'clock, Fritz returned to our house, and told us of his visit to the commune.

Lee, Buddy, and Fritz had gone to the address Cyndi had given them, finding it to be an old two-story house in a changing neighborhood of apartments and old homes in the shadow of the downtown district.

They decided that Lee and Buddy would wait outside, staying out of sight, while Fritz visited the commune.

Fritz went to the front door and knocked several times. Finally, a face peered from behind the curtain, and a young man motioned for Fritz to go around the back. At the back door, the man talked to Fritz for several minutes through the screen door. He told Fritz that Pennee was not there, but finally invited him in, locking the door behind them.

Fritz was admitted to a large, clean kitchen where the table was set, and the food was half-eaten on the plates. One by one, people began to reappear, and take their places at the table to finish their meal.

The house was old, with high ceilings, and worn wooden floors. From the kitchen Fritz could see into a bedroom. There were mattresses on the floor, and about ten young children were playing with toys in the middle of the floor. The house was sparsely furnished, and it was obvious that several families were living together in crowded conditions.

Someone got out a guitar, and they all began to sing songs about God that Fritz had never heard before. Then they all started chanting things like, "Thank you, Jesus, Thank you, God." They said these things over and over, louder and louder. Fritz was uncomfortable, and got up and told them he would be going now, but he'd come back tomorrow to talk some more.

Lee and Buddy, who had been waiting at the back of the house, heard a young woman, or girl, crying. They heard sounds like slapping, and someone whimpering and crying. Lee wanted to go to her rescue, but decided to just stay out of the way.

We talked till the wee hours of the morning, getting to know Fritz better. He was a fine young man and his concern for his sister was apparent.

The next morning Fritz came over again. "I've been up all night thinking about this," he said. "The only thing to do is take Pennee from them by force. She can't stay with that bunch of weirdos. Cyndi's right. There's no other way but to grab her." Fritz ran his hand over his hair and paced back and forth in the kitchen, while I poured him a cup of coffee. "I don't know how she could do this to our folks," he said. "They've been so good to us. I'm going to get her back, then I'm going to wring her neck."

He drank a sip or two of coffee and said, "I have to plan how to kidnap her. You know how they operate, and I need some help. I won't ask you to go with us when I do it, but I want to run the plan by you anyway. Will you help me?"

Well, I was not sure I knew how to plan a kidnapping. The question of ethics in kidnapping kids from the cults was becoming quite an issue, and I didn't know about the morality of such an action. Bo had snatched Cyndi against her will, but that had not been a planned kidnapping. He just did what he felt was the only thing to do at the time. We were glad he did, too. But could I help people plan to kidnap a girl whom I didn't even know?

There's a saying at our church that the members should be ready to sing, preach, pray, or testify. But kidnapping? What had Dr. Mac gotten me into?

I wanted to help Fritz all I could. There was no other way I could see to get Pennee back. We had asked for wisdom, and Fritz and I were both sure that the Lord would give it to all of us.

Charlotte, Lee and Fritz all arranged to take a few days off from work and concentrate on locating Pennee, then getting her out of the cult. Pennee's older sister Sherry was called, and she flew up from Florida to be with her family.

Charlotte was a real go-getter, and she was on the phone with people all over the country inquiring about the Children of God. She got much the same information we had gotten when Cyndi was missing. She did get some additional names of people whose children had been involved. It was the same story over and over again. "You may never see your child again."

Charlotte was told by several people that day that Pennee had probably been taken out of town by now, especially after the confrontation with the police at the condominium and

Fritz's visit to the commune. However, I felt that Pennee was still in Atlanta. The Johs told me that Pennee had a paycheck due in a few days, and I was counting on the cult to keep Pennee in town until she collected her money.

I suggested that they call the airline Pennee worked for, and explain to her superiors what had happened. Pennee had indeed quit her job, but when the airline officials heard that she had been taken by a cult, her supervisor said they would hold her resignation, pending the outcome of their attempt to get her back.

We discussed the possibility of grabbing Pennee at the airline office when she went to pick up her check, and the airline personnel agreed to assist in that plan.

Shan Gastineau dropped by for a visit. When he met Fritz, and learned about Pennee, he offered to go with Fritz to the commune. I was concerned that Shan would be recognized by the members of the commune. He was one of the boys who had gone with Cyndi to get her things when she had left that same house just two and a half months earlier.

Pennee phoned Fritz later that day, and told him she was glad he had come by the commune the night before. She set up a meeting with him for that evening at the colony.

Fritz asked me, "Do you think I could get her out of there tonight somehow? Could we just take her by force?"

"That's not likely," I said. "There are so many of them. You'd be outnumbered and they'd have the police there before you could get her out. Then you'd have ruined your chances of seeing her again. I'd suggest that you just visit with her for now, and size up the situation, and her condition. Let's just take this one day at a time."

"It makes me mad that the police defend the Children of God's right to keep Pennee under their control, even though she's not thinking clearly, and has obviously undergone a personality change in just a few days. Where's the justice?" Fritz was pacing again.

Shan and Fritz left, and we were all praying that they could

106

somehow convince Pennee to leave with them.

Fritz came back to our house a few hours later and told us what had happened at the commune.

Twenty minutes after the two boys arrived at the colony, Pennee, Pilgrim, and Mary Magdalene appeared. Pennee was glad to see Fritz, and greeted him with a hug, and told him that she loved him. She also hugged Shan and told him that she loved him, though she had never seen him before. "I just have so much love for everyone," she said.

Fritz asked to talk to Pennee alone for a few minutes, and Pilgrim said they could go into a bedroom to talk, but Shan would have to wait in the living room.

In the privacy of the bedroom, Fritz tried to talk to Pennee about the hastiness of her decision, but she seemed unable to carry on a normal conversation.

Fritz said, "She seemed so nervous, kind of hyped-up. Yesterday she looked drugged, but she was almost super-charged tonight. I just couldn't get her to respond to my questions. She kept saying things like, 'It's so wonderful to be serving the Lord full-time. Unless you leave your father and mother and forsake all, you can't really serve God. This is the only way, Fritz.' " She told Fritz she had been praying he would come and join the family. She quoted Scripture and kept saying over and over, "I love you."

"She's really off the deep end," Fritz said. "It was all I could do to keep from grabbing her by the arm and dragging her out of there. We were outnumbered though, and I knew we'd never be able to do it."

While Fritz and Pennee were talking in the bedroom, Shan was visiting with the others in the living room. They badgered him with questions, and without waiting for his response, they quoted Scripture out of context to answer the question. Someone asked Shan what he was studying for, and Shan told him he was studying for the ministry.

Pilgrim snorted in disdain. "A systemite preacher!"

Shan was obviously not their favorite person, and his choice of vocation was among the most contemptible to the Children of God.

One of the men in the room had been looking at Shan rather intently the whole time. He said, "Have we ever met before?"

"Could be," Shan answered. "I get around a lot."

"I mean, have you ever been here before?"

Shan would not lie, so he said, "Yes, I was here a few months ago with a friend of mine."

"I thought so. You're one of the guys who ripped off one of our sisters."

"I was with Cyndi when she decided to leave the group, but she was not ripped off. She decided to leave."

Pilgrim, who was apparently the head-honcho, said, "We're going to have to ask you to leave. You're not welcome here."

Fritz, unable to get through to Pennee, came out of the bedroom just then. Fritz was told that he was welcome to stay, but Shan would have to leave.

"I'm ready to leave, too," Fritz said. "I'd really like to talk to you some more another day."

"Come *alone* the next time," Pilgrim told him.

"There's just no way to get her away from them at the commune," Fritz said. "We'll just have to watch the house, and when she comes out, and isn't so well-guarded, we'll grab her then."

Lee Joh, who had been a highly decorated air force fighter pilot during the Second World War, planned the rescue operation down to the last detail. We all prayed and came up with a plan we hoped would work. Every now and then someone would come up with a detail that was obviously inspired. The gifts of wisdom and knowledge were clearly in operation.

Lee asked his next door neighbor, Lou, to help with the rescue. Lee also enlisted the aid of his son-in-law, Steve. The four men, and Pennee's older sister, Sherry, would watch the commune, and when Pennee left, they would follow the car. When they got out of the car, Fritz would grab Pennee, and force her into the car, while Steve, with Pennee's extra set of car keys, would get in Pennee's car and drive away.

They would then bring Pennee to our house to avoid the police, who, we were sure, would be called. We knew they wouldn't let Pennee go without a fight, and we were prepared for that. We knew from experience that parents have no rights in cases like this. Cults can legally brainwash young people, and use the law to keep concerned parents from interfering.

The next morning, just as planned, the four men and Sherry drove to the colony and parked their car a short distance from the house so they couldn't be seen.

They watched the house for hours. People living in the neighborhood saw the car full of people sitting there so long and called the police. The police arrived, made all of them get out of the car, searched them and asked for identification.

They had no choice but to tell the two policemen what they were doing there. When the policemen heard the story about Pennee, they were very understanding. "We don't see you sitting here. Good luck."

The vigil continued for several more hours. At last a young man came out of the commune house. He looked up and down the street and then walked up and down in front of the house for several minutes. The rescue party started the car. In a few minutes, Pilgrim came out, looked up and down the street, and then motioned for Pennee and Mary Magdalene to come out. Pilgrim, driving Pennee's car, backed out of the driveway and turned the car in the opposite direction from the rescue party. Lee quickly turned the car around, and began to follow Pennee's car. They traveled through one of the busiest sections of Atlanta, and had a difficult time staying with Pennee's car. Fritz later told us that they went through red lights, made illegal turns, and took chances that could have caused an accident and brought the police on their trail.

Finally, after many miles, Pilgrim crossed the road and brought the car to a stop in a parking lot next to a busy four-lane highway. The rescue party also stopped, and Fritz got out, running across four lanes of heavy traffic, without looking either way.

Pilgrim, Mary Magdalene, and Pennee were out of the car now, walking away from it, when Fritz came running up to Pennee and grabbed her around the waist. Pennee hugged Fritz and seemed glad to see him. Lee made a U-turn in the middle of all the traffic, and pulled into the parking lot. Pilgrim shouted to Fritz to let Pennee go, and started to reach for him. Looking Pilgrim in the eye, Fritz said, "Don't try to stop me, don't even try."

Lee ran over to where Fritz and Pennee were, and drew back his fist to hit Pilgrim. Lou deflected the blow, saying, "We don't need that, we've got what we came for." Pilgrim glared at Lee, hate in his eyes.

Mary Magdalene, seeing that Pennee was being rescued, ran back to Pennee's car and tried to get back into it. She screamed as Steve pulled her from the car. As he struggled with her, Lee took the keys, and got into Pennee's car. Lee had never driven the Volkswagen before, and he couldn't get it in reverse, so he just drove over the curb, and out into the traffic, not looking either way. Fritz led Pennee to the waiting car and she got in and greeted Sherry with a hug. They took off, leaving a furious Pilgrim and Mary Magdalene in the parking lot.

Chapter 14

Charlotte and I had waited by the phone all day, she at her house, and I at mine. We talked a few times, briefly, not wanting to tie up the lines in case they tried to call.

It was Charlotte's birthday and she said the best gift she could have would be to have her daughter returned safely to her.

About three that Thursday afternoon a car pulled into my driveway. Lee came to the door looking tired and drawn. "We have Pennee," he said. "She's in pretty bad shape. She won't get out of the car."

"Come on in," I said. "You call Charlotte and tell her that Pennee is here. I'll go out to the car and meet her. The police will probably be at your house with a warrant for you in a little while. I'm sure Pilgrim has called them by now."

I walked out to the car. Fritz was trying to persuade Pennee to get out of the car and come inside. I put my head in the car and met Sherry and Pennee. Pennee was clinging to her older sister like a frightened child. Sherry gave me a warm smile, and said, "I'm glad to meet you." Sherry had that same beautiful smile, and pretty blonde hair that her mother had.

Pennee eyed me suspiciously. "Who are you?" she asked.

"I'm a friend of your parents," I said. "I've heard a lot about you, Pennee."

"My name is Rebecca," she said firmly. "Please don't call me Pennee."

"Okay, Rebecca, would you like to come in and have a cup of tea, or coffee or something?"

"I don't drink things like that. Only water and milk. I keep myself from all impure things. That's scriptural, you know."

She began to look something up in the Bible she was holding, her hands shaking as she flipped through the pages. She was not able to find what she was looking for, and I thought she was going to cry.

"That's all right," I said gently. "We'll look it up later."

She looked at me and said, "I'm just a babe, you know. I've learned a lot in the last few days, but I have so much more to learn."

She had such a childlike quality about her. She was a pretty girl with dark hair, and wide hazel eyes fringed with dark lashes. She wore no make-up, and her curly hair was pulled back in a pony tail and tied with a scarf. A few wisps of hair had fallen loose and were in tendrils around her face. She looked thin and fragile. She was dressed in wool slacks and a print blouse, topped by a sweater. My immediate impression was that this girl had lovely clothes, and wore them well. I tried to see beyond this recently acquired austerity to the person that was Pennee.

"Let's go in and visit with Lee for a few minutes," Sherry suggested. Pennee closed her eyes, and shook her head.

"Are you afraid of me?" I asked her.

"I just don't know you," she said. She looked at me as if she were trying to see into my soul. "Are you a Christian?" she asked.

"Yes, I am."

"A lot of people think that they're Christians, but they really aren't," she said, her eyes narrowing.

"I suppose you're right," I said. "Why don't we go inside and you can tell me what you've learned these last few days."

She looked at Sherry, and smiled. "I love you," she said, and she hugged Sherry.

This girl was really on some kind of a trip. There was just no getting through to her.

I wondered what to do next. How would we get this strange, beautiful girl out of the car? What would we do with her when we did get her out? I prayed silently.

The school bus stopped at the corner and the children got off and started coming down the street. Eric was one of the first off the bus. He saw the crowd in our driveway and came running over to the car and said, "Hi, mom, what's going on?"

"Hi, Eric. These are two of Fritz's sisters." I started to introduce him.

Pennee sat up straight and smiled a bright, big smile at Eric. "What a beautiful child!" she said. "Is this your little boy?"

"Yes, this is Eric."

She got out of the car and went over to Eric and hugged him. "You're so cute," she said. She stood there with her arms around Eric, smiling. "I just love children," she told me, smoothing his hair. "You have such pretty blond hair," she said to him.

The neighborhood children who had gotten off the bus were walking very slowly by our house now, looking at us curiously. Eric gave a sidelong glance at his friends going past. He didn't like to be hugged privately, and public hugging was out of the question. He looked at me as if to say, "How can I get out of this?"

Then he looked up at Pennee, and I could see compassion in his eyes. He seemed to realize that this was a special situation.

"Let's all go in the house," I said brightly.

Pennee stepped back from Eric, fear in her eyes. I thought she might run.

Eric took her by the hand and said, "Come in my house with me." She allowed Eric to lead her up the walk, onto the porch, and in the front door. They sat on the couch and looked at his school papers. Pennee did not seem to be aware of anyone but him.

Wendy and Amy came in and I introduced the girls to everyone. Pennee hugged both girls and told them she loved them. Then I took all three children into the kitchen. "This is kind of an unusual situation," I explained. "It would be helpful if you would get yourself a snack, and then go outside to play for a while."

"What's wrong with that girl?" Amy asked. "Why does she talk so funny? Is that Fritz's sister that you've been talking about?"

"Yes, Fritz got her away from the Children of God this afternoon."

Wendy asked, "Will she be like that for a long time? Does she usually talk like that and hug everyone and say I love you?"

"I don't think so," I said. "She's been through a lot the past few days, and she's not herself right now."

"I don't like the Children of God," Amy announced. "They made Cyndi not like herself too. They're not very nice, are they?"

The phone interrupted my answer to Amy. It was Charlotte, wondering what the situation was at our house, and how Pennee was doing now.

"They've really done a job on her," I said. "She's not able to respond to questions in a normal way at all. It's as if she's been programmed with Scripture, and pat answers. She's giving them out like a recording."

"Is she in worse condition than Cyndi was when she was taken from the group?"

I hesitated a moment before answering. I didn't want to add to Charlotte's worry, but she needed to know her condition. "I'm afraid she's somewhat less in touch with reality than Cyndi was."

"Do you think she needs to go to the hospital?"

"Well, she's really spaced out. If she were my daughter I would take her immediately to the doctor and let him decide."

Charlotte said she would call the psychiatrist who had treated Cyndi, and see if he could see Pennee right away. "Let your younger children come over here and stay with me while you're dealing with Pennee," she suggested.

I agreed, and someone came and took the three youngest children over to the Johs house.

Back in the living room, Pennee refused to drink or eat anything offered her, even though the rest of us were having iced tea or coffee. She insisted that we all sit on the floor rather than on the furniture. "I've gotten used to sitting on the floor," she explained. "People are too soft these days, too used to luxury." So we all sat on the floor.

"I'd like to share my testimony with all of you," she said.

She began a long, rather incoherent story of meeting Pilgrim and Mary Magdalene in the ice cream parlor, and her decision to serve God one hundred percent. Pennee had a hard time keeping her mind on what she was trying to say. She rambled on and on, changing the subject often, and becoming confused. If anyone asked her a question, she would shake violently, and stop to pray aloud, asking God to help her give her testimony. She paged through the Bible, her hands trembling, looking for Scripture to give credibility to what she was saying. She referred to the rest of us in the room as "lost souls in need of salvation." She was here, she said, to tell us about God.

I looked at her as she sat there cross-legged on the floor, reading out of the Bible, and I had a hard time seeing the vivacious, bright young woman that her family had described to me. This girl had been an airline stewardess for years, had done well in school, had many friends, and had been self-sufficient, yet close to her parents. Now here she was, renouncing her family, her country, her job, and pledging her loyalty to a group that she had learned of only a few days earlier. It was incredible what could happen to a person in just a few days.

She was so shaky that we tried not to upset her any further. She seemed to be hanging on by a thread. We were all very gentle with her, and just went along with whatever she said.

Cyndi came in and I introduced her to Pennee and Sherry. Cyndi joined us on the floor, as if it were the most natural thing in the world for her to come home and find everyone sitting in the middle of the floor reading the Bible.

"I was in the Children of God for a while," Cyndi told Pennee.

"Did you get taken from them by force too?" she asked, looking accusingly at Fritz.

"The first time I went in, my boyfriend grabbed me, and my parents took me home. Then I went back to the family after a few months, but I came out on my own the second time. That was just a couple of months ago."

Pennee drew back from her, as if she had just been told that Cyndi had the plague.

"You left the family? You just left them of your own free will?" She was incredulous.

The phone had been ringing like mad the whole time we were talking. Lisa and Julie had come in too, but when they saw everyone in the living room, they elected to stay out of the way. I was called to the phone and Charlotte told me that she had talked to the doctor. He would see Pennee in his office as soon as we could get her there.

I came back to the living room to find Cyndi telling Pennee how she felt about the Children of God. "They're not what they claim to be," Cyndi said. "Mo is a false prophet, preaching a doctrine of hate. They really messed up my mind for a while. I'm just glad I'm out. You'll be glad too, later."

Pennee was trying to find something in the Bible to show Cyndi. She couldn't find what she was looking for, and she started to shake again. She bowed her head and chanted in a whisper, "Thank you, Jesus, thank you, God, thank you, Jesus, thank you, God." She bounced her head up and down slightly in rhythm to her chanting.

Cyndi reached over and took Pennee's hand. "Don't do that!" she ordered. "You're keeping yourself hypnotized when you do that. Don't chant!"

Cyndi was not being as gentle with Pennee as the rest of us, and Pennee had become much more upset since Cyndi had

116

come home. She was shaking badly now.

"Let's not talk about that right now," I said. I shook my head signaling for Cyndi not to talk to Pennee.

Sherry had been talking to her mother on the phone about taking Pennee to the doctor. "We're going to go see a doctor, Pennee," Sherry said.

"No," Pennee said quietly. She picked up her Bible again and started flipping through the pages.

Glen came in from the business trip he had been on that day. When I introduced him to Pennee, she jumped to her feet, and put her arms around Glen. "I love you," she said.

"Well, what a nice warm greeting after a hard day," Glen answered. He was unruffled by the strange behavior of Pennee and the houseful of strangers sitting on the floor.

The doorbell rang, and Shan Gastineau, and his father, Gene, were there. Gene and his wife, Pat, were good friends, and they, and the rest of our Bible study group had been praying about Pennee for days. They were checking, Gene said, to see how things were going. They had not been able to get us on the phone. Our line had stayed busy all afternoon.

With everyone standing now, I thought this might be a good time to get Pennee to go out to the car with us.

"We were just about to leave, to take Pennee to see a doctor friend of ours," I told Gene and Shan. I didn't look at Pennee to see her reaction, but just proceeded as if we were all agreed.

"I'm not going," Pennee said. "I need to pray now."

She began to pray, but she couldn't continue, and started to cry. Gene took over for her. He prayed aloud, binding Satan from interfering in this situation in the name of Jesus.

I looked at Sherry and Fritz, and said, "Let's go." They each took one of Pennee's arms, and led her out of the door.

"Let's go in my car," Glen said. "I know where the doctor's office is, so I'll drive. It's kind of tricky to find unless you've gotten lost a few times."

The doctor greeted us in the waiting room, and met Pennee. It was after office hours, and he had been waiting for us for some time. He asked Pennee if she would come into his office with him for a few minutes, and she took his arm and went along like he was an old friend.

The rest of us stayed in the waiting room, talking about our unusual day. Sherry, Fritz, and Steve told us of their encounter with the police, being "frisked," the bizarre chase, and the rescue. It all seemed like something out of a novel.

"Someday this might all be funny," Sherry said. Fritz said he thought it was funny already.

Sherry and Steve questioned us about our experience with Cyndi and the Children of God. We answered their questions, and tried to reassure them. "Even though Pennee seems so far from the real world now, I'm sure that she'll recover just as Cyndi has," Glen said.

"Cyndi really seems sharp, and perfectly well now," Sherry said. "That gives me hope for Pennee."

After about an hour the doctor and Pennee came out of the office. "Pennee has agreed to sign herself into the hospital for a few days," he told Sherry.

Pennee just smiled and nodded, seeming much more relaxed now.

Looking at Fritz, Sherry said, "Why don't you and Steve take Pennee out to the car while I make arrangements about the hospital."

Sherry motioned for me to come to where she and the doctor were standing, as the rest of the party went out the door. "What exactly is wrong with Pennee?" Sherry asked the doctor.

"Well, she's out of touch with reality."

"What do you mean by that?"

"I really don't like labels," he said, "but if you're looking for one, we could say quite accurately that she's psychotic at this time. Tomorrow she may not qualify for that label, however."

Dr. Beckman had treated Cyndi when she came out of the cult, and he was familiar, in a limited way, with the aftereffects of the cult's brainwashing.

"We're just learning about how to deal with patients coming

out of these religious cults," he told us. "It's a new phenomenon in the field of psychiatry. All we know is that these young people act much the same as men returning from POW camps. We're dealing with intense mind control, and behavior modification. It's kind of brainwashing, really."

We drove Pennee to the hospital where she signed herself in. She seemed very calm now, but as if she had been drugged. She was smiling that fixed smile, and her eyes were glassy. She moved about her hospital room as if in a trance. She walked over to the window chanting softly to herself, and knew she had the rest of the world tuned out.

Sherry asked her what she would like to have brought to her. Pennee just smiled and said, "I don't need much now. I've found true happiness."

Sherry made a list: Toothbrush, nightgown, cosmetics. "Anything else?" Sherry asked. Pennee just smiled at her, not answering.

We left Pennee there with a nurse. Sherry told her that she would return in a short while with her overnight bag.

We were all relieved that Pennee was rescued from the Children of God, but all of us knew her ordeal was far from over.

Chapter 15

Riding home, we didn't talk very much. It had been an emotionally and physically exhausting day.

We were all amazed at how everything had turned out. It was as if pieces of a puzzle had fallen perfectly into place, one by one, until the rescue had been completed. We knew the hand of the Lord had moved each piece into place at just the right time.

When we got home, we learned that the police had come to the Johs house with a warrant for Mr. Joh. Pilgrim had signed a complaint stating that the Johs had kidnapped Pennee, and stolen his personal possessions.

Charlotte told the police that her husband was not home. Their daughter had been rescued, she told them, not kidnapped. She explained that Pennee had been with a man and woman from a cult who had had Pennee in their complete control, and who had apparently brainwashed their daughter. She explained that Pennee was now under the care of a doctor. The policemen thanked Charlotte, and told her that since Pennee was safe, and under the care of a doctor, they would not need to serve the papers on Lee.

Later that night in the kitchen, Lee put his arms around Charlotte. "This wasn't much of a birthday for you," he said, tears welling up in his eyes, "but you did get what you asked for. Our daughter is safe. When I drew back my fist to strike Pilgrim, he looked at me, and the whites of his eyes turned red.

I'll never forget that as long as I live. I felt as if I were looking into the eyes of a snake." Lee shuddered as he recalled it.

The following day, while going through Pennee's car, the Johs discovered the car was packed and ready for a trip. There was also a great deal of information about the Children of God.

We could see why Pilgrim was concerned about his possessions. There were lists of people's real names, their biblical names, their present locations, and the names of their parents. There were manuals on brainwashing, pills, files, Mo letters, tapes, and documents marked "for leaders only."

We looked through these things, realizing that we had come upon some pretty damaging evidence about the cult's methods. These Mo letters were not the seemingly innocent "you gotta be a baby" variety, but were hate-filled tirades against America, the church, and a variety of other institutions. Some of them were sexual, some political. They had a pro-Communist slant.

As I looked through these Mo letters, I noticed that in almost all of them there was a cartoon of a lion looking on, or participating in one way or another in the picture.

"What is this lion all about?" I asked. Cyndi, who had been looking over the material with us, said, "Oh, the lion is Mo. He always depicts himself as a lion in the Mo letters."

"How appropriate," I said. I remembered the Scripture that says, "Satan prowls like a roaring lion, seeking whom he may devour." "He's devouring our young people," I said, "and he's doing it under the guise of religion."

I was learning a lot. I never thought we could be deceived by someone who claimed that Jesus Christ is Lord, but these people were doing it. They were deceiving even the Christians. I hadn't thought it was possible to use the name of Jesus for deception.

The Johs sought legal counsel. On the advice of their doctor and lawyer, Lee Joh was made Pennee's legal guardian for ninety days. This would provide the Johs with the legal right to take Pennee away from the cult, should they find her, and take her back again. This also provided an added measure of security at the hospital. They turned the things found in Pennee's car over to the deputy attorney general.

We felt sure that Pilgrim would try to find Pennee, and try to get her to come back. She was in no state of mind to make any important decisions right now. Her father would make them for her for a few months. This would also protect Pennee's possessions. We knew from previous experience that by now she had probably signed over her car, and given her power of attorney to the shepherd. This was standard procedure for the cult.

Pennee was extremely unhappy in the hospital. She called her parents several times every day to complain about her situation, and every day when they came to visit her, she begged them to take her home. Her Bible had been taken from her, and she was told by the hospital staff that she was not to talk about God or Jesus.

Though the doctor taking care of Pennee was a Christian, his visits to her were brief and took place only once a day. The psychiatric aides taking care of the patients, however, were not necessarily Christians, and their influence was constant. During group therapy, Pennee was told that a fear of spiders indicated an overbearing mother in one's background. If one had a fear of horses, that indicated a fear of one's father. Freudian theories were expounded day and night. Pennee was required to participate in yoga, and encouraged to try meditation.

All of this disturbed her very much. One of the other patients told Pennee that if she ever wanted to get out of there, that she better quit talking about God, and just go along with the program whether she liked it or not.

The Johs did not want Pennee involved in a cult, but neither did they want Pennee's faith in the Lord to be undermined or discouraged. They were at a loss to know what to do.

Pennee had some good days and some bad days in the hospital. Charlotte had good days and bad days too. We did a lot of talking and sharing during those weeks, getting to know each other better than most people would in years of casual friendship. We really got close to the whole family.

Cyndi and Charlotte were good friends from the first meeting, and I was glad that Cyndi had someone like Charlotte to talk to. Charlotte remarked several times that Cyndi was such a comfort to their family. "If Cyndi could recover so beautifully, Pennee can too."

Charlotte and Lee talked to many other families whose children had been involved in the Children of God. A doctor in Florida, whose daughter had been involved a year earlier, talked with them on the phone several times. He felt that Pennee would not really recover until she had been deprogrammed. He also pointed out the danger of Pennee returning to the cult if she were not deprogrammed.

When Pennee had been in the hospital about two and a half weeks, the Johs came to visit her as usual, and found that she had packed all of her things and was ready to go home. She had been begging every day to be taken home, but now she was crying.

"If you leave me in here, I will go crazy!" she sobbed. She was crying so pitifully her parents didn't know what to do with her. "I'll even talk to a deprogrammer. I'll be deprogrammed if you want me to, just get me out of here."

Lee and Charlotte talked it over, and decided that Pennee was not getting any better in the hospital. Maybe a deprogrammer was the answer. They decided to take Pennee home and contact the deprogrammer we had talked to on the phone when Cyndi came out of the cult.

Charlotte and Lee took every precaution to prevent Pennee from slipping away in the middle of the night. Charlotte slept with her, and barely closed her eyes all night. Pennee was full of fear. Every sound made her shake and tremble. She was sure that the devil was after her because she was away from the calling of God. She had been taught in the cult that when one left the group, you were open to attacks from Satan. People who left, she believed, would surely die.

Charlotte and I talked on the phone the next day, about having Pennee deprogrammed. I had negative feelings about deprogramming, but Pennee was their child, and it was their decision. I could understand how desperate they were. If psychiatry was not helping Pennee, then perhaps the deprogrammer would.

The deprogrammer was in another state, working with a family whose son had been with the Sun Myung Moon's group for a year. They reached him by phone, and arranged to have Pennee deprogrammed in a few days.

Later we talked with the Johs about Pennee's scheduled deprogramming. Lee asked, "What made you decide against deprogramming for Cyndi?"

Glen said, "I just couldn't get any straight answers from the deprogrammer I talked to on the phone. I asked him what deprogramming was, and he gave me vague answers about shooting holes in the walls that Children of God had built up in Cyndi's mind. When I asked him how he shot these holes, he was evasive and gave me a lot of double talk. He also wanted a thousand dollars for his services. He later said he could deprogram her for five hundred dollars since no air fare would be involved. He wanted to take Cyndi away from home for a week or more. He told us that there would be a rehabilitation period after the deprogramming. I didn't like the sound of any of it. I questioned him about his relationship with the Lord, and he was vague and evasive on this point too. He warned us that if Cyndi were not deprogrammed, she would still be under the influence of the Children of God, and she might go back with them again. She did go back, as you know, so maybe deprogramming is necessary. I really don't know what to tell you."

The third day Pennee was home from the hospital, Cyndi and Charlotte went to the airport to get Dave Brubaker, the deprogrammer.

They came directly to our house since Dave felt it would be

125

better not to meet Pennee till he had set a time and place for the deprogramming.

When I was introduced to Dave, the first person I thought of was Obadiah. He looked like the young man in the commune in Chattanooga where we had gone the previous summer to get Cyndi. Dave was taller but had that same thin, gangly look. He had a crop of brown, curly hair, and his horn-rimmed glasses were bigger than any I had ever seen before, and they sat perched on his upturned nose, looking as if they might slide off. He kept pushing them up with his middle finger every few minutes.

Dave asked Glen and me if he could deprogram Pennee at our house. He explained that it was never a good idea to do the deprogramming at the Children of God member's own home. "Sometimes people don't like to recall the deprogramming. They feel they were confined against their will, and it makes them uncomfortable to be in those surroundings later on."

We told him that we'd have to know more about it before we could give him an answer. We had many questions.

We went into the living room to talk. Dave sat on the couch, slid down on his spine, folded his hands across his chest, crossed his legs, and gave us a bored look over his glasses. He looked as if he were facing a very unpleasant situation and he was going to endure it, and get it over with as quickly as possible.

"What would you be doing, exactly?" Glen asked.

"I will tell Pennee that we will be talking about the different cults, how they manipulate the mind, and break it down to the point where they can begin to program the new recruit with their doctrine. Then I will explain to her what the Children of God believe, and why it's in error."

"Pennee has a strong faith in the Lord, and her parents would not like that to be undermined, or put down in any way," Glen said.

"Yes, sir," Dave said, looking very bored.

"You are then prepared to give her the truth to take the place of the lies she's been told. Is that right?"

"Yes, sir."

"Just what is the truth as far as you're concerned? Are you a Christian?"

"Yes, sir."

"How long have you been a Christian?" I asked.

"Since high school."

Getting information from Dave was like pulling teeth. He was obviously not happy about being questioned about his methods, or his faith, but we felt that these were important questions. We had known the Johs less than a month but we had grown very close to them. We interviewed Dave as if he would be dealing with our own child. We wanted to know exactly what would be going on in our home.

"How long would it take to deprogram her?" I asked.

"It varies. Sometimes it takes a week or more, sometimes just a few days."

"Is there anything physical involved in a deprogramming?" I asked. "I saw a movie a few years back about a deprogramming, and it was pretty brutal."

"That was a crock," he said. "Nothing like that goes on."

"I just want it clearly understood that Pennee is not to be touched, or threatened, or restrained in any way, do you understand?" Glen was looking at him with one of his most serious expressions.

Dave sat up a little straighter now, hearing Glen's firm tone. "No sir," Dave said. "I won't touch her, or anything."

"Would you prevent her from sleeping or eating or do anything at all to make her uncomfortable?" I asked.

"No ma'am."

Glen and I looked at each other. "Would it be all right with you, Lee?" Glen asked me. "You're the one who would be directly involved with it."

I wanted to do all I could to help the Johs. Pennee wanted to be deprogrammed. In fact, she was anxious to get her mind back to normal again.

"You can do it here," I said.

"This is kind of unusual," Dave told us. "Most of the people I deprogram don't walk into it willingly."

"Pennee's an unusual girl," I said. "She knows she needs some answers, and she's smart enough to want to get herself back to normal as quickly as possible, even if it means deprogramming. That takes a lot of courage."

Dave asked Cyndi to help him. "It's good to have a girl who's been in the cult helping when I'm deprogramming a girl," he said. "There are some things it's easier for them to talk about to another girl."

It was decided that the deprogramming would begin that evening. Fritz was out of town, so Charlotte and Lee were going to stay the night, just to be nearby. Dave wanted a member of the family to be there. "Sometimes the person being deprogrammed tries to run out of the house," he said, and he wanted a member of the family to be there to prevent her from leaving if she should try. It was usually not a good idea for the parents to play that role, he said, but since Fritz was out of town, Lee and Charlotte were elected.

Dave and Pennee were in the downstairs bedroom, with Cyndi observing, when they started by going over the definition of a cult. They established that Children of God was a cult. Then they got into the techniques used by all the cults to brainwash their members.

About eleven o'clock, the doorbell rang, and there was Fritz! He was needed for the deprogramming, and the Lord had worked it out so he could be here instead of on the job he was scheduled to do. Charlotte and Lee went home, and Fritz was there all night, while Pennee was deprogrammed.

True to his word, Dave used no physical force, or threats. She was allowed to sleep when she wanted to, and when she woke up, they began where they left off, with tapes, and facts about the cult, and conversation about why these groups were wrong.

Glen and I had gone to bed when the Johs left, leaving the situation in Fritz's capable hands.

About six in the morning, we were wakened by Pennee laughing almost hysterically. The laughter was infectious, and Dave, Cyndi, and Fritz were laughing too. Glen and I came downstairs to see what was happening. Dave explained that when a person is deprogrammed they frequently come to a place where they cry hysterically, in relief, or, as in this case, they laugh. It's the breaking point, he said, and the person is deprogrammed when they come to this place of emotional release.

Pennee was sitting up in the bed, saying, "It's so silly, it's so funny. Now I see how they do it."

Well, I didn't think it was at all funny. What the cult's brainwashing methods do to the mind is no joke, but Pennee was really laughing in relief. She was glad to be released from the mental prison the cult had locked her into.

We all had a big breakfast, and talked about what had gone on the night before. I still didn't understand how Dave had brought Pennee to this point, but I was glad that Dave considered her deprogrammed.

Cyndi said, "I think the deprogramming did just as much for me as it did for Pennee. Now I have a better understanding of what they did to me up in Chattanooga, and how they did it."

They were now going to begin the part of the deprogramming called "rehabilitation." Cyndi, Dave and Pennee would spend the next week together, doing things like going out to eat, seeing movies, and just having fun.

The next few days were really wild. Besides our own six children, there was Pennee and Dave, and when Fritz was in town, he was there too. The phone rang so often I couldn't keep up with it. People were so glad that their prayers had been answered.

Charlotte came in with enough groceries to feed an army, and cooked a big ham dinner with all the trimmings. When I protested, she just said, "Please let me do this, Lee. I need to help."

Dave, who had been in the Children of God for five and a half years, told us of the difficult time he had during this rehabilitation period. He was unable to make even the simplest decisions. He couldn't order a meal in a restaurant, or decide what clothes to buy. He had been programmed not to think and to allow the shepherd to do his thinking for him.

Dave encouraged Pennee to make small purchases, order meals or snacks in a restaurant, and decide what she wanted to do with her time. They went to movies, shopping, and to the park.

Dave was still anti-church and, we felt, anti-parent. Charlotte and I discussed this, and we were both concerned that perhaps he was having a somewhat negative effect on the girls. We felt that after five years or more of such intense indoctrination, he was not completely over the teaching and attitudes held by the group.

Charlotte said, "You can take the boy out of the cult, but you can't take the cult out of the boy after that many years." He had said many things to the girls that bothered us. He made derogatory comments about the government, about organized churches, and parental influence on young people. We were all relieved when his work was finished.

Chapter 16

Pennee progressed nicely, continuing under the care of a psychiatrist. We saw her almost every day, and we could see there was a continual, gradual improvement in her condition. By now, Cyndi and Pennee had become good friends.

Charlotte and I laughed several times about our girls listening to the other one's mother, but not her own. I remarked to Charlotte once, "It's amusing. I can make a comment to Cyndi about something, and there's no response. You say the same thing, and it's a pearl of wisdom." Charlotte told me she felt Pennee was much more open, and communicative with me than with her.

Charlotte and I were told over and over by many people, whose children had been in cults and by psychiatrists, that it takes a minimum of one year for young people to get over the effects of the cult's brainwashing. It was hard to believe that, but we were finding with our own girls that it was true. When Charlotte was having a bad day, I would remind her that her year was not up, and when I had a bad day, she would remind me. The Lord had really given us this special friendship not only with each other, but with our daughters as well.

Pennee was asked to speak to a group of doctors in Florida as part of a panel which was to be made up of former cult members. Pennee accepted the invitation and began to prepare for it by going over the Children of God material. Charlotte could see this was having a bad effect on her. The

Johs suggested that perhaps it was too soon for Pennee to be trying to do this, but she wanted to help others by getting the information out. She continued to study the material and prepare for the seminar.

But reliving the experience and going over the Mo letters proved to be too much of an emotional strain for Pennee, and she had a relapse. She was again hospitalized, but this time it was at a different hospital.

In this hospital, Pennee was allowed to read her Bible, and she could talk about her faith in the Lord without being put down, or made to feel that she was odd for having such beliefs. There was even a chapel for the patients to visit if they chose to. This time she was quite content in the hospital, and she was released after two weeks, feeling more like her old self than she had in a long time.

Spring had come, and Charlotte and I were sitting on her back porch, enjoying the beautiful weather. The dogwood and azaleas were at their peak, and we were glad the long, hard winter was behind us. We could always share whatever was on our minds, and it was nice being so comfortable with each other.

"You know, Lee," Charlotte said. "Whenever I heard of kids getting off the beaten path, or getting into a jam of any kind, I always thought their parents must have failed them in some way. I don't believe that any more. I had raised four children before Pennee, and never had much worry with any of them. Then all of this cult business came into our lives. I've changed my attitude about a lot of things these past months."

"I know what you mean," I said. "I used to think I had the perfect formula for raising children, one that was guaranteed to keep you from problems. Take them to church, keep them busy, set a good example, give them a home unbroken by divorce, listen to them, love them, and the Lord would protect you from all problems. I guess we've both learned a lot this year. I still believe in my formula, but now I know there are no guarantees."

Cyndi and Pennee were together a lot during that summer. Pennee spent as much time at our house as her own, and we loved having her. We all had a sense of humor, and we laughed a lot. Pennee and Cyndi were talking more and more about parental influence on their lives. Frequently they would discuss their childhood, commenting on their similar upbringing. They both seemed to feel their parents had made a lot of mistakes, and they let us know what they were. Charlotte and I were compared too, and not always favorably. Of course, Cyndi thought that even though Charlotte and I were a lot alike, Charlotte was not as bad as me. Pennee allowed that we were alike. But I was always the heroine with Pennee.

I let these criticisms pass without much comment, but it was beginning to get to me. The girls always seemed to have a reason why they sometimes used bad judgment, but it was always someone else's fault, never their own.

One day they were playing "My mother is bossier than yours." I was listening to this for the umpteenth time, and I was really tired of it. They were both saying that their mothers tried to run their lives, and never let them make decisions for themselves.

"Just hold on a minute now," I said. "I've been hearing you girls talk like this for a long time, and I've always kept quiet. But I think you've been on this kick for too long. If you girls think that Charlotte and I get our jollies by trying to run the lives of our grown-up kids, you don't know us very well. If you girls would stop trying to pass the buck and lay the blame for every problem you have on your parents, you'd be a lot better off. That's what I'd call a Freudian cop-out.

"All either of us wants is for you two to get your heads together, and be independent, well-integrated adults. We don't want babies in grown-up bodies. Pennee, your mother is a sharp lady with a career of her own, and a husband that she'd like to spend some time with. She'd like to quit worrying about you.

"And as for you Cyndi, I still have five younger children at home to raise, and I'd like to give them and your father more of my time and attention."

I was currently reading Jay Adams' book *Competent to Counsel*, and I said, "Excuse me a minute. I want to read something to you." I left the room to find the book, leaving them sitting there looking very surprised. I came back to the room with the book, having found the portion I was looking for. Jay Adams was quoting from a folk song by Anna Russell:

I went to my psychiatrist to be psychoanalyzed
To find out why I killed the cat and blacked my
husband's eyes.
He laid me on a downy couch to see what he could
find,
And here is what he dredged up from my
subconscious mind:
When I was one, my mommie hid my dolly in a
trunk,
And so it follows naturally that I am always drunk.
When I was two, I saw my father kiss the maid one
day,
And that is why I suffer now from kleptomania.
At three, I had the feeling of ambivalence toward my
brothers,
And so it follows naturally I poison all my lovers.
But I am happy; now I've learned the lesson this has
taught;
That everything I do that's wrong is someone else's
fault.

They just sat there for a minute, amused by the poem I read them. Cyndi looked at Pennee and said, "I think we've been told off." They said the poem was very amusing, but it didn't apply to them. They were being treated like infants by their parents and they didn't like it.

"You've both been acting like little spoiled girls for a long time now," I said. Everyone is aware that you've both been through a terrible experience, and it's been hard getting yourselves back to the people you were before your meeting with the Children of God, but I for one am tired of it. Everyone has been treating you with kid gloves. We've been pussyfooting around, taking your verbal abuse, afraid to offend you.

"You sleep till noon, stay out late, play tennis, swim, and just lead a life of loafing and complaining. You're acting like little children, but you want to be treated like adults. You want all the privileges of an adult, and none of the responsibilities. You can't have it both ways. If you want to be treated like adults, act like adults. If you want to continue to act like children, then be prepared to take the supervision that children need. I think you should start contributing to the upkeep of the home, and you Cyndi, are going to start paying room and board, and helping around here with the housework."

They sat there, looking at me, their eyes wide with surprise. Pennee laughed, and came over and hugged me. "You really can have a fit when you get mad, can't you? You're usually so sweet, and sympathetic, but you really can lose your cool!"

They left to go for a walk, chuckling and talking as they walked up the driveway. They might think it's very funny, I thought, but I meant every word I said.

I didn't know what Pennee's situation would be, but I made a decision that day to start demanding more from Cyndi. It came down to "shape up, or ship out."

I talked to Charlotte on the phone later, and told her what I had said to the girls. "I hope I didn't offend Pennee too much," I said, "but they've had it coming for a long time. It felt good to tell them how I really feel about things." I shared the poem with Charlotte from *Competent to Counsel*.

"You're absolutely right," she said. "I'm glad you told them what you thought. I hope they both listened and will make an effort to do something about their attitude. When you finish that book, I'd like to borrow it. It sounds like it could be very helpful. Don't worry about offending Pennee. Your friendship is solid enough to withstand some differences of opinion. I feel exactly the way you do. I've had it, too. I think we both should tell our girls that there will be some changes made."

The girls were told they'd have to start making some contributions to the family. They would have to adjust their schedules and life style to fit in with the rest of us. They would be expected to help around the house, and pay a small sum for room and board.

This was not a popular innovation with either of them. Pennee had been living with her parents since her rescue, and she decided that this was a good time to move back to the condominium with Fritz.

Cyndi, who was still in school, and did not have a good job like Pennee, did some shaping up. She also began to make plans to get a job in the near future, and possibly get an apartment. It was a start toward maturity.

Chapter 17

A young man called us one evening, telling us he had heard about us from several people. He told me he and his wife had both been in the Children of God for a long time, and they would like to share some things with us. I invited them to come to our house the following day.

Jack and Connie Wasson looked like flower children. Jack was tall and well-built, with a full brown beard. His hair was beginning to thin slightly. Connie was short and softly rounded, with a pretty, angelic looking face. She was wearing a long peasant-type dress, and she had on no make-up or jewelry. They both had a well-scrubbed, fresh look, and their two little blond boys were clean and well-behaved.

They told us the Lord was leading them to start a retreat home where young people could come to rest and recuperate after leaving the Children of God, or any other cult.

They told us of their long struggle to get their minds and spiritual lives back into focus after leaving the group in Amsterdam more than a year and a half earlier.

"What made you leave the group?" we asked.

Jack did most of the talking, and told us that Connie had been one of the original twelve members of the Children of God, when they began in California, and had more information about the group than anyone else outside the family. Jack had been with them for several years, he said. He had been an ordained minister working with Teen Challenge before joining the Children of God.

We were amazed that this intelligent, articulate young man could be talked into joining a far-out cult. We listened intently as he told his story of becoming disillusioned with the organized church, and the church's inability to meet the needs of young people. He had joined the group in Philadelphia, he said and had been very enthusiastic about the ministry of the Children of God. He was particularly interested in getting young people off drugs, and onto Jesus.

Some time later, he met Connie, and they were married. Jack went on to tell us of his travels with the group, and of his growing concern about the inconsistencies and scriptural misinterpretations presented by David Berg. Jack challenged some of the teaching in the Mo letters and fell into disfavor.

Mo decided that Connie and Jack had grown too close, and wanted to send one of them to another colony. Jack and Connie both resisted that idea. There was a growing policy within the family, they told us, to break up married couples who seemed to love each other very deeply. They were "putting each other before Christ," Mo said, and had to be separated for the good of the whole body. Connie and Jack were very troubled about their situation. They talked about leaving, but they still believed in the ministry, and only wanted to get away to think things through for a while.

Jack had challenged some of Mo's teachings, and had been thinking on his own. This, coupled with the fact that Connie knew so much about the cult from its beginning, was apparently a threat to Mo. Mo could not receive any negative feedback at all, and was dismissing all who questioned his teaching.

Jack also came to realize that the "angels," who were supposedly ministering to the group were "familiar spirits."

This really got our undivided attention.

"What do you mean?" we asked.

Jack explained, "During our prayer time, we would ask for guidance, and spirits began to manifest themselves to us, and give us information about things that would be happening in the next few days."

"What kind of things?" Glen asked.

"Just small things really, like when someone would be getting a letter, or when a check would be coming, or prophecies about personal matters. After these spirits had been visiting us regularly for a while, we all felt terribly depressed. The joy seemed to be gone from our worship. Then one day, I just prayed that the Lord would lift the spirit of depression, and in the name of Jesus, I bound Satan from interfering in our lives. The 'messengers' never returned. This troubled us. At first, we thought we must have some unconfessed sin in our lives. We prayed in earnest that the Lord would reveal those things to us so we could confess them and get a right relationship with Him again. Then came the revelation that the 'angels' were familiar spirits, and we had, in effect, been conducting seances. When I told the others what I had discovered, I was thought to be a troublemaker.

"Connie and I left the group then. Temporarily, we thought, just to think things over, and to pray that the Lord would bring the ministry to a pure salvation message."

Jack and Connie told of being on their own in a foreign country. They told us of months of confusion and depression. They felt as if they were struggling for their very sanity.

Later, the Wassons met a man in England who had been a big contributor to the ministry, but who had become disillusioned with the group, and had withdrawn his support. He gave Jack a huge book containing computer print-out pages of names and addresses of members, and former members. There was information about each member, including their cult name, their real name, and names and addresses of parents and other relatives. This lengthy list included the names and addresses of those who had left the group, and why.

Jack and Connie wrote letters to every parent and every person who had left the group, and told of their desire to start a ministry to help young people back on the road to sanity.

Jack showed us some of the letters he had received from the parents, and some letters from the former members themselves. They were so much the same. People told of their long struggle back to a normal life, the loneliness, and inability to cope with even the most routine details of living. Some told of leaving a husband or wife in the family, and the sorrow of the separation. The regret over broken marriages was very sad to read about. There was a letter from a young woman who left with two small children, telling of her struggle to earn a living for the three of them. Her parents had disowned her and would not help her in any way, or even see her.

The saddest letters were those from parents whose children had returned, but had committed suicide after leaving the group. I was troubled to see this was not uncommon. We could see that Jack and Connie had a vision for a much needed ministry.

Jack took a book out of his briefcase.

He handed it to me and said, "Since this is the place to come for help and information in the Atlanta area, you should have the whole story. This has become a corrupt and diabolical group, and you should know just how far they have fallen. You're writing a book on the subject, and you need to see this."

I looked at the book he placed in my lap. It was written by Moses David, the cover said, and the title was *Free Sex*. I paged through it, very gingerly, prepared for the worst. That's what I got. It was illustrated in the typical comic book style of Mo letters I had seen before and it seemed to be a compilation of Mo letters put into book form. I saw the one Cyndi had been shown in the colony called *Women in Love* which taught that it was perfectly all right to have a homosexual relationship, but just between women. Mo contended that the Bible only spoke against male homosexual relationships.

Jack paged through the book pointing out other letters on sex. I was shocked by what I saw. I had never seen anything like it in my life. I read quickly over the text of the letters, not wanting to read them in detail. I was embarrassed and shocked.

The drawings were pornographic, which was bad enough, but the blasphemy that accompanied them was more than I could believe. The titles of the letters told the story. One had a mermaid on the cover. It advocated flirting and instructed the cult members in the art of being "bait" for the cause. "Do what you must to attract new converts to the family," it said.

Another letter had a drawing of a shapely girl, with a fishhook through her body. The title of this one was *Hookers for Jesus*. I was disgusted with looking at the book, and closed it and handed it to Jack.

"I don't want to see any more," I told him.

Jack handed it back to me. "Don't read the letters, just look at the illustrations, and the titles."

"This is supposed to be inspired by the Lord?" I asked. "What kind of people would believe such filth is from God? How can intelligent people like you be made to believe that any of this could be divine inspiration? It's straight from the pit."

"One is not given this sort of thing the first week in the group. It's so gradual, so subtle. The members are fed one bit of deception, then another, and another, and little by little, they can't discern the truth any longer," said Jack.

Glen paged through the book, shaking his head in disbelief. "This is the filthiest thing I've ever seen. It's pornographic blasphemy."

Jack agreed. "It's hard to believe how far the Children of God have fallen. David Berg is obsessed with sex, and he's promoting it in the name of religion. It wasn't this way until recently, you understand. In the early days, it was straight gospel. No monkey business at all. The disciples were brought in with the true salvation message, and no one tolerated sexual misconduct, not even Mo. It's getting worse and worse and worse all the time. The really straight kids coming in now, especially those who know the Bible, like Cyndi, leave when confronted with this trash. The others who've been in the group for years, are under the bondage of deception. They justify it somehow and stay in."

141

We were grateful to the Wassons for helping us to understand more about the Children of God. We could now see that God protected His own even within the group, if they were serious and followed Him alone, and we knew that Christians who were firmly grounded in Scripture were those least likely to be deceived by David Berg and his teachings. But those who were not Christians, and knew no Scripture, but who were searching for something worthy of their commitment were always in danger of being taken in.

Chapter 18

Cyndi came in from work one day just before Thanksgiving, and told us she would be going to South Carolina for the holiday. "I'm going with Dave to help him deprogram a girl who's been with the Children of God for about six months or so. Her mother has arranged for us to come up there tomorrow and start right away."

I didn't like this at all. It was just like Dave to call Cyndi at work about this, and not at home. "You're not going to talk this over with your father first?" I asked.

"No."

This is typical of Dave's influence on her, I thought. I'm just not going to argue with her about it.

"I hope you don't plan to get involved in kidnapping her, or imprisoning her against her will."

"No, she's already home. She came for the holiday. All we have to do is lock the door, and deprogram her. I've been wanting to see a real deprogramming anyway. Dave says that Pennee's deprogramming was a piece of cake. She walked in wanting to be deprogrammed, and it was not at all typical. I want to know the true story, and I want to help other people get out of the cults."

"Well, you know how I feel about deprogramming, and I want you to know that I don't approve of you going off with Dave."

"I'm not asking for your approval, I'm just telling you where

I'll be for Thanksgiving."

I was really irritated with Cyndi, but I didn't want to get into an argument with her, so I got in the car, and drove to the store, hoping I'd feel a little cooler when I got home. Maybe Glen could talk some sense into her. She was sure more than I could handle.

Glen came home from work, and I told him what Cyndi was planning. He voiced his disapproval, but she went anyway. We were worried about her going off to deprogram some strange girl with a young man we did not approve of. We were worried about her safety. What if the young woman became violent? What kind of home was she going to? What kind of people were they? Cyndi took our questions as interference, and could not seem to understand our concern for her safety.

When Cyndi returned several days later, she had the girl with her. They would be together for the rehabilitation part of the deprogramming. Dave had arranged for Cyndi and Allison to stay with a friend of his for a week. He never showed his face at our home, but dropped the girls off and scooted out of our driveway fast.

Allison was a bright girl of twenty. She was not spaced out as most of the ex-cult members we had seen. She did not chant, or quote Mo letters. We talked a lot the next few days. Allison was open and eager to tell me about her experiences in the cult, and her deprogramming. When they came by each day, they would share a little more with me.

Allison had been a full-fledged member of Children of God for about six months, but had been what is called a "catacomb" member for more than a year before going to live in the colony. She explained that she went to all the meetings and parties, and had received instruction and indoctrination from the shepherd. Their influence on her had been in effect for a year and a half.

I asked Allison how she felt about being deprogrammed.

"I was really mad when I realized I was being deprogrammed. I was scared, too. You know what we're taught

144

in the family about deprogramming. When I realized I was locked in, and Cyndi and Dave were deprogrammers, I panicked. I felt betrayed and tricked by my mother."

"How do you feel about it now?"

"I'm glad I have the truth about the group, but there must be a better way to get that information to people. Deprogramming is a pretty frightening experience."

Cyndi said, "I'm never going on another deprogramming, it was just awful."

"Can you tell me about it? I really would like to know what goes on. Pennee's deprogramming is the only one I've ever been involved in, and that was done under the close supervision of Pennee's family, and ours. I'd like you to start at the beginning, and tell me what happened, if it wouldn't be too painful for you."

Allison said she wouldn't mind sharing with me. She told me that she was at her cousin's apartment, and Cyndi and Dave were there. They were introduced as friends of her cousin, and they visited for a while, then they played a game. After they had been together for about an hour or so, the friends who had brought her there said they would have to leave for a while, and they would return for Allison a little later. Dave then locked the door and told Allison that she was going to be deprogrammed.

"What did you do then?"

"I started to cry. I was really scared. I screamed, and hit Dave, and beat on my cousin. I was really violent, I guess. I wanted to run, but I knew I couldn't get out of there. I felt like a trapped animal."

"Did they hurt you in any way? You said before that it was an unpleasant experience."

"That's an understatement. It was degrading, humiliating, and frightening. Dave yelled at me, and called me names, and told me that we would take three months if necessary to get me to reject Mo and his teachings. I didn't want to stay there three months, so I stopped crying, and listened to what he was saying."

145

"What kind of names did he call you?" I asked.

Allison said, "He told me I was a whore for David Berg, and when I told him I was not, he said that every time I brought a new member into the family, I was acting as a prostitute. Several times Cyndi stopped him from yelling at me and calling me names. I couldn't have taken it without her help. I felt like she was on my side. The things she told me really helped more than anything. She just gently told me what the group was really all about. I believed her, and appreciated her kindness."

Cyndi listened to all of this without much comment.

"Cyndi, do you feel that Allison has told it pretty much the way it happened?" I asked.

"That was it all right. It was bad news. I'm never going on another deprogramming. I feel that so much more could be accomplished with love and gentleness. No one needs that kind of scene. Dave was awful."

Cyndi spent the next week with Allison, taking her to movies, shopping, and other activities that would help her adjust to the world outside the cult.

The girls stopped by the house after a trip to the drug store. Allison was in another room, and Cyndi told me that she had spent over an hour in the drug store, encouraging Allison to choose her own hand lotion. "She wanted me to make the decision for her, but I told her to take her time, and pick it out herself. She looked at all the hand lotions in the store, and couldn't make a decision. I finally picked out three or four, and told her to pick from those. She kept saying, 'Just any one will do.' It was really hard for her to pick out hand lotion. Can you believe that?"

"Did she finally pick it out herself?" I asked.

"Yes, but only after I told her that we were not going to buy any unless she picked it out herself. I started for the door, and she just grabbed one off the counter, and bought it."

When she ate with us, she would never state a preference for tea or coffee with her meal. "Whatever" seemed to be her favorite word.

146

Allison was an intelligent, articulate young woman, but she needed to have this rehabilitation time. I could see that, and I could understand better now the kind of ministry that would be required to really help these young people as they freed themselves from the grip of the cults.

Chapter 19

There were more and more invitations coming asking me to speak to women's groups, churches, and schools. I marveled so many times at the changes brought into our lives by our brief encounters with the Children of God. I was not a public speaker, but people were interested in the growing involvement of our young people in the cults. We had lived through it, and people wanted to hear firsthand what happened and how we managed to get our daughter back. It was an opportunity to expose the cults, but it was also an opportunity to tell of the amazing power of the Lord, and His help and very real presence in our time of need. We could not have done it without Him, and I said so every time I spoke to a group.

After I told briefly about our experience, I would give the audience an opportunity to ask questions. There seemed to be a number of questions that were asked over and over.

The question of deprogramming came up almost everytime I spoke.

We had met a young man named Tousey Wilson, who had been deprogrammed by a well-known deprogrammer.

Tousey told us at our earlier meeting that he would be glad to tell us sometime about his deprogramming.

I called his wife Rebecca and asked her and Tousey to come by and share with us at their convenience. I asked her if it would be all right to invite Charlotte Joh to hear their story. Charlotte had been speaking at churches and schools too, and people called her from time to time for help. I was sure she would want this information too. Tousey and Becky agreed to meet with us the following Saturday.

Tousey was tall and slender with a crop of dark hair. He had a serious, scholarly look, but he smiled easily as he spoke. Rebecca was tiny and her long brown hair was pulled back in barrettes. She was dressed in jeans and a shirt. It was hard to believe she was the mother of two children.

Tousey and Rebecca spent the whole afternoon with us, and the story they told was both interesting and enlightening.

After serving coffee and cookies, I asked them to tell us how they had become involved with the Children of God, and how long each of them had been in the group.

Tousey told us that he was one of the many people involved in a house ministry here in Atlanta called the House of Judah. That ministry had been infiltrated and taken over by the Children of God. He joined the Children of God then and had been in the cult for four years. I had heard many times before about the House of Judah. In fact, most of the young people from the Atlanta area who had joined the Children of God in the early seventies were originally connected with that house ministry.

Rebecca told us that she was in nurses' training in Colorado and dropped out of school to join the Children of God there. She told us of her upbringing as a Roman Catholic, and her conversion experience while she was in school. She described the people there in Colorado as sweet and beautiful people, who seemed to have such a love for the Lord and mankind that she joined them. She told of the peaceful mountain retreat owned by the Children of God, and the wonderful fellowship she found there. She loved the Bible studies, and felt sure that God had called her to serve Him full-time and learn more about His word in this way.

"I was in charge of the print shop, and took care of all the printed material for the Children of God distributed in the western hemisphere," Tousey told us. "Rebecca worked as a

150

translator. Having been raised in South America for some of her childhood, she speaks and writes Spanish fluently. Rebecca and I were legally married, not just by the shepherd, as is sometimes the case."

Charlotte asked, "Did you choose each other, or was your marriage arranged by the leaders?"

Rebecca and Tousey answered together, "We chose each other."

They went on, Tousey continuing to tell his story.

"We had a unique situation there in Puerto Rico. Everyone in the colony had a highly specialized skill, so we didn't have the transient type of life style that is typical of the group. We had all been together for a long time, and things were run in a much more relaxed manner. We talked things over, and questioned pieces of material that we thought to be off base in some way. We would walk down to the coffee shop nearby, and talk things over and raise questions. I know now that this was unheard of in other colonies."

"What kind of things did you question?" I asked.

"When all that sex stuff started coming out, we were pretty surprised, and we talked it over openly, and challenged it within our own group."

"When did the material start to change?" I asked.

"I think it was the letter called *Mountain Maid* that first got me thinking that things were not quite right with Mo."

I thought back, and I remembered seeing the letter *Mountain Maid* among the Mo letters in Pennee's car the day after her rescue.

There was a drawing of a pretty girl with long blonde hair. She was topless, and holding a big basket of flowers. She was supposed to represent the new free woman. On the back of the letter there was a hard looking woman wearing a bra and lots of make-up, her hair combed into a tortured teased and sprayed style. She represented the "systemite woman."

Tousey said, "I questioned the merit of such a publication. How could this possibly be edifying to anyone? This letter was

151

selling like crazy in North America, but it was banned in all of South America. We would have been put in jail for distributing anything like that there. The Mo letters just got worse and worse, and you know what they've come to now. Jack showed you some of the latest pieces of trash."

I nodded, remembering that *Free Sex* book.

"Then Mo started coming out with prophecies that never came to pass. I was rapidly losing faith in Mo and the ministry of the Children of God. I talked things over with Rebecca, and we went to another colony where my brother was living in Puerto Rico, just to talk over these questions with him."

"What was his reaction to your questions?"

"He just said though we didn't understand these things now, in time we would see these were important letters. He was firmly behind Mo, all the way."

"We were all invited to come home for a visit" Tousey went on. "My brother, Rebecca and I and our little girl were all going home together for a family reunion in Florida. We were going to meet at my grandparents' beach house."

"Had you kept in touch with your parents during those four years since you'd joined the group?" I asked.

"Yes, we wrote pretty regularly."

"Had they given their approval when you and your brother joined?"

"No, in fact they were very upset, and voiced their disapproval in the beginning, but after we were in for a while, they never said anything against it again. That's why we were so trusting, and went home for a visit."

"When did you realize you were going to be deprogrammed? Was the deprogrammer there when you came in?"

"No, Dave was there. We had known him in the family, and we didn't think too much about it when we came in. We just visited with him for a while. We didn't know he had been deprogrammed and now was helping to deprogram other people. We were sitting there visiting, my whole family in the room. My parents, my grandparents, my aunts and uncles. All

152

of a sudden Dave sat up and said, 'Okay, let's cut the crap.' "

"I was a little irritated that he would talk like that in front of my family, and I told him to cool it. Then he started with stuff like, 'David Berg is a false prophet.' He got into what sounded like a memorized dissertation on the evils of the Children of God."

"How did you react to these statements?" I asked.

"We just laughed at him," Rebecca said.

"Two more men came in then and we knew we were going to be deprogrammed," said Tousey. "We might have been able to laugh at Dave, but this was no laughing matter."

"How did you feel when you saw them? Were you afraid?"

"I was terrified," she said. "I wanted to run. I knew we were in for a rough time. Tousey just said, 'Oh, no. How could my folks be doing this?' "

The deprogrammer began by using the foulest language we'd ever heard to describe David Berg and his followers," Tousey said. "He just went on and on. My brother asked 'Are we being held here against our wills? If not, I would like to go for a walk on the beach.' He got up and walked toward the door. When he was almost to the door, the big burly man who had come in with the deprogrammer jumped up, grabbed my skinny brother and literally threw him across the room. Then the deprogrammer jumped on him and grabbed him around the throat. I sat there watching all of this, the big guy watching me, to see if I would make a move to help my brother. I knew we couldn't fight this, so I just sat there."

"What were your parents and the rest of your family doing while the deprogrammer was on top of your brother, choking him?" I asked. I couldn't imagine people just watching that sort of thing without trying to stop it.

"My parents were programmed to accept this sort of thing. The deprogrammer talks to the family members first, and tells them there will be violence involved. They are told they must not interfere, it's part of the deprogramming. He finally let my brother up, and we all sat down again. The deprogrammer looked at us, and said, 'If I have to keep you here for six months, I'll do it. We'll be together until you reject Mo and his teachings.' "

"Did you believe he'd keep you confined that long?"

"We believed him. He was wild, and we were afraid of him.

"A woman deprogrammer came with them, and they told us we would have to be separated now. Rebecca and the baby would be going with my parents and the woman."

Rebecca took over the story there. "I was determined not to leave my husband. I told them I didn't want to go without Tousey. The deprogrammer said, 'You're not legally married to him, anyway.' We told him we had been married by the head of the supreme court in Puerto Rico. The judge was a friend of ours, we told him. This really seemed to come as a surprise to everyone. Then he said, 'Okay, just take the kid.' The man who had thrown my brother-in-law across the room was walking toward the crib where our baby was sleeping. They intended to send her somewhere with Tousey's parents. I really panicked and said, 'Wait, I'll go with you. I can't leave my little girl.'

"We were taken to a hotel, where they had rented two adjoining rooms. The lady deprogrammer was pleasant, and she just talked to me. I was not threatened or hurt in any way, but I was watched very carefully. I was planning my escape all the while. I planned to write a note, and pass it to the waitress when we went to the dining room. They brought the meal up to the room, however, and so I tried to think of another way to get out. I just acted very calm, and went along with what the lady was telling me. I heard the lady tell my mother-in-law in the next room, 'I think she's coming out of it.' She thought I was being deprogrammed.

"I put the baby down for a nap, and lay down next to her pretending to sleep. Everyone was in the next room with a door between the two rooms open. I very quietly slipped out of the door, ran down the hall and called the police, telling them I was being held against my will, and would need their help in getting my baby back, and having my husband rescued.

154

"The police arrived, and I got the baby, and went with the police to the beach house. It was empty. They had been called and had moved to a hotel.

"I was taken to a home for delinquent girls, where I remained for the next few days, trying without success to locate Tousey and his brother. I finally decided to go home to my parents in St. Louis for a few days, till Tousey could be freed and get in touch with me. It was two weeks later when we were reunited."

"What went on during those two weeks, Tousey?" I asked.

"We were taken to a hotel far out of town after the warning call, and held there for the next week. We got more of the same vulgar tirades and threats of lengthy imprisonment if we didn't come around to their way of thinking.

"The deprogrammer did most of the talking. He told my brother and me we were just a couple of beggars living on donations, not working for a living.

"We decided to start talking back to him. 'How do you earn a living for your family?' I asked him.

" 'My expenses are paid by families like yours whose kids I straighten out. I also get donations to help with additional expenses,' " he told us.

" 'What's so different about your line of work and ours? We both live on donations,' my brother said.

"He got furious. I thought he might get physical again, so we decided to cool the arguing, and just go along with the program.

"They played tapes to us. They badgered us with facts and figures about the Children of God, and David Berg. They defined the word cult. They called the Catholic and the Episcopal churches cults. They attacked and belittled everything concerning the Children of God. We pretended to agree with them, just so we could get out of there.

"Finally, we were returned to our parents, supposedly deprogrammed. We were disgusted. We felt we had been betrayed by our own family.

"We agreed to take jobs, and work for three months. We were also forced to sign a paper stating we would not press charges against anyone involved with the deprogramming.

"Rebecca and I were reunited, and we rented an apartment in Atlanta, and I got a job. My brother took a job too, just to prove to the family that he was not brainwashed, and was functioning normally. His intention from the beginning was to return to the Children of God after the three month period.

"My intention to leave the commune before the deprogramming, was reevaluated. Rebecca and I were planning to leave anyway, but now we were so angry, we thought maybe we should go back if this is what the systemite world had to offer. Our counter-culture life style was more peaceful than this mess.

"Rebecca was determined to go back to the group in Puerto Rico. The man who was the shepherd of the colony in Puerto Rico was a close friend, and he wrote to us, encouraging us to return. Then he wrote to just Rebecca, asking her if she was going to follow me or the Lord."

Rebecca said, "This was a rough time for me. I knew my brother-in-law was going back, and I wanted to go back too, but Tousey was my husband and I loved him. The teaching in the family was that you should forsake your partner if there was a question of loyalty to the group. Nothing should be put above the group, not even your husband. Well, I really had to do a lot of praying. I was at a crossroad and I went to the Lord. He showed me that he expected me to be submissive to my own husband. I decided to stay with Tousey, and submit myself to him 'as unto the Lord.' It was the best decision I ever made."

"What happened during the next few months?" I asked.

"It was a terrible time for all of us. We were depressed and confused. We were also angry with our parents for having us deprogrammed."

"Didn't you think they had undertaken this illegal and expensive deprogramming for your own good, because they loved you?"

"It was pretty hard for me to accept that. I was coming out anyway, and I don't feel it did anything for me, except to make me angry."

"How do you feel about your parents now, two years after the deprogramming," Charlotte asked.

"The Lord has really been good," Tousey said. "In the natural, I suppose both of us would still feel badly toward my parents because of their part in our deprogramming. But we don't. Right now both Rebecca and I enjoy a very close and loving relationship with my parents. We really praise the Lord for it."

"What happened to your brother? Did he go back to the Children of God?"

"Yes. He worked for three months first. My parents asked him to hold down a regular job for that period of time, to prove he was not brainwashed. When this three months was up, he rejoined the Children of God, and my parents have not heard from him since."

"How do you feel about the Children of God now?" I asked. "What about Moses David?"

Rebecca said, "I think Mo really got off the track when he divorced his wife and married his secretary. He would never admit he had sinned in this matter. He defended his action instead of confessing it, and getting right with the Lord, so that sin just grew, and obsessed him, and corrupted his ministry."

Tousey added, "His latest Mo letters are worse than any I had seen before. All of them are about his secretary's affairs. She's being a 'hooker' to win people to the Lord, Mo says. It's really sick. One of the saddest things I know is that Mo turned out to be a false prophet. Young people so desperately wanted a godly man to follow."

Tousey and Rebecca told us of the terrible struggle to get their minds and spiritual lives back to normal. They, like all of the others I had talked to, said it took about a year.

"You obviously feel very bitter about your experience, and would not recommend deprogramming, is that right?" I asked.

157

"Right!" they both said.

"Well, what is the answer to getting kids out then? You were about to leave anyway, but what about those who are not as spiritually discerning as you are? Should they be left in the cults to continue in their spiritual prisons? What would you recommend for parents facing this question?"

"Love is the answer, not force. I would recommend that a parent who knows his child is in a cult just keep in touch with their child by letter, letting them know you love them. Ask them to come home for a visit, and when they're home have a former cult member talk to them. Not to deprogram them, just talk. If it's done in a spirit of love and concern, this will come through, and will have an effect on the person. Love is the greatest weapon we have against the cults."

Cyndi had come in while we were talking to Tousey, and she sat there, listening to the last few minutes of what he had to say.

"I think you're right," she said. "The second time I went in, I went with my guard up, wary of everything they told me. When I read that *Women in Love* Mo letter, I knew how wrong they were, and that I had to leave, but I didn't think I could go home. I thought I'd hurt my parents too much, and they wouldn't want me back. Then when I went to pick up my check, and my mother's letter was waiting, telling me she loved me, and I could come home any time, I cried my eyes out. I think it was really the love of my parents that brought me out. The love and concern shown by Todd and Rhys, coming all the way from Athens just to see me really touched me, too. The Lord must really love me a lot to surround me with such loving, caring friends.

"I would have really resented being deprogrammed. I agree with you, Tousey, especially after taking part in a deprogramming myself. Love really is the better way."

Epilogue

Newspapers and magazines are full of stories about deprogramming. On the one hand, we can have empathy with the parents of young people caught in the snare of the cults. However, it is still a violation of the First Amendment to take a person against their will and have them deprogrammed. Recently, in two separate articles, appeared the story of a young man who joined a Catholic order of monks, and his parents had him kidnapped and deprogrammed. A Catholic nun was also deprogrammed after leaving the Protestant religion of her parents. My question is, who decides who needs deprogramming and who doesn't? I fear this new trend may be taken to extremes.

Parents are now bringing their children out of the cults legally by using a law that has been on the books for many years. Under this plan, parents sue for a thirty-day "conservatorship" over even adult offspring, using laws designed mainly to protect the senile from fraud. Once out of the cult, distraught parents have no recourse but to have the child deprogrammed by experts. The cost for this service can range from ten to twenty-five thousand dollars. But what of the child after the deprogramming? Has he or she been given something to fill that void in their lives?

Jesus tells us in Matthew 12:43, "When the unclean spirit has gone out of a man, he [the spirit] passes through waterless places seeking rest, but he finds none. Then he says, 'I will

159

return to my house from which I came.' And when he comes he finds it empty, swept and put in order. Then he goes and brings with him seven other spirits more evil than himself, and they enter and dwell there; and the last state of that man becomes worse than the first."

There are so many evil forces coming against us today. Not only the cults, but things like astrology, scientology, Edgar Cayce, and his reincarnation doctrine, Transcendental Meditation, Yoga, ouija boards, and witchcraft, to name a few. All these things are Satan's tools to capture the minds of our young and old alike. That's where the battle really is; in the mind.

In these last days, when God is pouring out His spirit so abundantly on His people, Satan is coming against us in great power, trying to defeat the church, and rob us of victory. But that does not mean we have to be cowering victims, powerless against this deceiver. The Scriptures tell us that "Greater is he that is in you than he that is in the world." And "Where sin [Satan], does abound, there does grace [God's love], more abundantly abound. We need never be fearful; only aware of the enemy. And with that awareness, should be the awareness of who we are in Christ.

People often ask me what we can do to stop the cults from spreading and prospering. The answer is so simple, I almost hesitate to say it. People should stop handing out money to groups soliciting on the streets, in parking lots, airports, and wherever these young people are out asking for donations. All most people need to hear is that these kids are with a "Christian Youth Organization," and people dig down in their pockets and hand them some money. If Americans would stop this good-intentioned but irresponsible support of the cults, they could not continue. They depend on the panhandling of young people to keep their movements going.

Exposure of the real motives and beliefs of the cults is another method we have to fight the spread of this cancer.

Our churches could come against the cults by exposing the

groups in Sunday school, and at youth meetings. Our kids are really ignorant of what the cults are all about, and in that ignorance there is danger.

Whenever I speak to a group, the question is always asked, "What makes kids join these cults?"

I've asked every ex-cult member I've talked to that question, and the answer is always the same. They're searching for a deeper meaning to life. They want a total commitment to something they can believe in.

Our churches are not offering our young people what they are longing for in the way of fellowship, leadership, and teaching. We don't ask our kids, or anyone, to make a total commitment. They see our churches as watered down, lukewarm "churchianity." This does not interest, excite, or challenge our young people.

Glen and I began working with young people in churches when we were not much older than college age ourselves, and I know how tough it is to get a viable program going. Just getting the word out that there's life there in the church takes time. But with prayer and hard work, it can happen. It takes work and planning, and committed leadership.

Our materialistic society has left our young people hungry for something spiritual to illuminate their lives. They want a group they can belong to, people who really care about them. A way to serve the Lord. They have not found, even in our churches, an outlet for their idealism. They meet these cult members who tell them they've found the answers to all their questions, and they invite them to come with them to learn more.

Our children are following these Pied Pipers who play the tune that says, *Come away with us. Leave this world of jobs, and pressures, and things, and parents. We'll think for you, we'll take care of you, you'll have a place where you belong. Love is here, come follow us.*

We parents look for the enemy that is stealing our children. We look in the communes, and we can't find the enemy. Surely the enemy is not these sweet children. Then we look to the leaders of the cult. They must be the enemy, surely. We say that Sun Myung Moon is the enemy, or Moses David is the enemy. We don't get to meet the leaders, so we imagine they are the enemy.

The enemy who is disrupting the family today is that same enemy who disrupted the first family in that garden where God had so beautifully established them. The Bible tells us that we "wrestle not against flesh and blood, but against principalities, and powers and rulers in high places." Our battle is not with Moon, or David Berg, or any of these other deceivers, but in the realm of the spirit world.

As Christians, we must begin to put on the armor of Christ, and take the offensive against these evil spirits that would come against us. We have in Christ a risen Savior, a victorious God. The battle is already won by Him, and we need to arm ourselves with the word, we need to pray, we need to claim the victory that is ours by using the power that is available to us today. That same mighty power that raised Christ from the dead is available to us now. We just have to ask for it!

If we don't want our kids to join the cults, we must offer them appealing alternatives. If we fail to offer the only alternative, which is the knowledge of the power of a risen Lord, we, like the townsfolk of Hamelin, will see our children follow one Pied Piper or another through the doorway in the mountain, until they're all in, never to be seen again.